Also by Tom Cooper:
A@W Volumes 13, 14, 18, 19, 21, 23 & 24

Also by Albert Grandolini:
A@W Volume 19 & 21

Also by Arnaud Delalande:
A@W Volume 19 & 21

Published by
Helion & Company Limited
26 Willow Road, Solihull, West Midlands,
B91 1UE, England
Tel. 0121 705 3393
Fax 0121 711 4075
Email: info@helion.co.uk
Website: www.helion.co.uk
Twitter: @helionbooks
Visit our blog http://blog.helion.co.uk/

Designed and typeset by Kerrin Cocks,
SA Publishing Services
kerrincocks@gmail.com
Cover design by Paul Hewitt,
Battlefield Design
www.battlefield-design.co.uk
Printed by Henry Ling Ltd, Dorchester,
Dorset

Text © Tom Cooper, Albert Grandolini &
Arnaud Delalande, 2016
Monochrome images sourced by the authors
Colour profiles & maps © Tom Cooper, 2016

Cover: An F-14A Tomcat from VF-74 Be-
Devillers is about to be launched from one
of two bow catapults on the aircraft carrier
USS *Saratoga* (CV-60) the off Libyan coast
in early 1986. (US Navy Photo)

ISBN 978-1-910294-53-6

British Library Cataloguing-in-Publication
Data.

A catalogue record for this book is available
from the British Library.

For details of other military history titles
published by Helion & Company
Limited contact the above address, or visit
our website: http://www.helion.co.uk.
We always welcome receiving book
proposals from prospective authors.

CONTENTS

Note

In order to simplify the use of this book, all names, locations and geographic designations are as provided in *The Times World Atlas*, or other traditionally accepted major sources of reference, as of the time of described events. Similarly, Arabic names are romanised and transcripted rather than transliterated. For example: the definite article al- before words starting with 'sun letters' is given as pronounced instead of simply as al- (which is the usual practice for non-Arabic speakers in most English-language literature and media). For easier understanding of ranks of French Air Force and US Navy officers cited in this book, herewith a table comparing these with ranks in the Royal Air Force (United Kingdom):

Royal Air Force (United Kingdom)	Armée de l'Air (France)	US Navy (United States of America)
Marshal of the RAF	général d'armée aérienne	Fleet Admiral
Air Chief Marshal (ACM)	général de corps aérien	Admiral (Adm)
Air Marshal (AM)	général de division aérienne	Vice Admiral (V-Adm)
Air Vice Marshal (AVM)	général de brigade aérienne	Rear Admiral (Upper Half)
Air Commodore (Air Cdre)	Colonel (Col)	Rear Admiral (Lower Half)
Group Captain (Gp Capt)	Lieutenant-Colonel (Lt Col)	Captain (Capt)
Wing Commander (Wg Cdr)	Commandant (Cdt)	Commander (Cdr)
Squadron Leader (Sqn Ldr)	Commandant d'escadron	Lieutenant Commander (Lt Cdr)
Flight Lieutenant (Flt Lt)	Capitaine (Capt)	Lieutenant (Lt)
Flying Officer (Flg Off/FO)	Lieutenant (Lt)	Lieutenant Junior Grade (Lt JG)
Pilot Officer (Plt Off/PO)	Sous-Lieutenant (S-Lt)	Ensign (Ens)
Chief Warrant Officer (WO)	Aspirant (Asp) /Major[1]	Master Chief Petty Officer

GLOSSARY

4WD	Four-wheel drive
AA	anti-aircraft
AAM	air-to-air missile
AB	Air Base
AdA	Armée de l'Air (French Air Force)
AEW	Airborne early warning
ALI	Aero Leasing Italiana
AMI	Aeronautica Militare Italiana (Italian Air Force)
AML	Automitrailleuse Légère (class of wheeled armoured cars manufactured by Panhard)
APC	Armoured Personnel Carrier
ATGM	anti-tank guided missile
AWACS	Airborne Early Warning & Control System
BVR	Beyond visual range
CAP	Combat Air Patrol
CBU	cluster bomb unit
CG	Cruiser, Guided (hull classification for US Navy's cruisers armed with guided missiles)
CIA	Central Intelligence Agency (USA)
c/n	construction number
COIN	counterinsurgency
CV	Carrier, Vertical (hull classification for US Navy's aircraft carriers)
CVBG	Carrier Battle Group
CVN	Carrier, Vertical, Nuclear (hull classification for US Navy's nuclear-powered aircraft carriers)
CVW	Carrier, Vertical, Wing (composite carrier air wings embarked on board USN carriers)
DD	Destroyer (hull classification for US Navy's destroyers)
DDG	Destroyer, Guided (hull classification for US Navy's destroyers armed with guided missiles)
EAF	Egyptian Air Force (official title since 1972)
EC	Escadre de Chasse (Fighter Wing)
ECM	Electronic countermeasures
ELINT	Electronic intelligence

FANT	Forces Armées Nationales Tchadiennes (National Army of Chad)
FIR	Flight Information Region
FROLINAT	Front de Libération Nationale du Tchad (National Liberation Front of Chad)
FSLN	Frente Sandinista de Liberación Nacional (Sandinista National Liberation Front)
GUNT	Gouvernement d'Union Nationale de Transition (Transitional National Government of Chad)
HQ	headquarters
IADS	integrated air defence system
IAP	International Airport
IDF/AF	Israeli Defence Force/Air Force
IFV	Infantry fighting vehicle
Il	Ilyushin (the design bureau led by Sergey Vladimirovich Ilyushin, also known as OKB-39)
Km	kilometre
LAAF	Libyan Arab Air Force
MANPADS	man-portable air defence system(s) – light surface-to-air missile system that can be carried and deployed in combat by a single soldier
MBT	Main Battle Tank
Mi	Mil (Soviet/Russian helicopter designer and manufacturer)
MiG	Mikoyan i Gurevich (the design bureau led by Artyom Ivanovich Mikoyan and Mikhail Iosifovich Gurevich, also known as OKB-155 or MMZ 'Zenit')
MPA	maritime patrol aircraft
MRL	Multiple rocket launcher
NADGE	NATO Air Defence Ground Environment
NATO	North Atlantic Treaty Organization
NCO	Non-commissioned officer
NODA	Nucleo Operativo di Difesa Aerea (Air Defence Operation Cell)

NSC	National Security Council
OCU	Operational Conversion Unit
RPG	Rocket Propelled Grenade
RWR	Radar Warning Receiver
SA-6 Gainful	ASCC codename for ZRK-SD Kub/Kvadrat, Soviet SAM system
SA-7 Grail	ASCC codename for 9K32 Strela-2, Soviet MANPADS
SAM	surface-to-air missile
SEPECAT	Société Européenne de Production de l'Avion d'École de Combat et d'Appui Tactique European Company for the Production of a Combat Trainer and Tactical Support Aircraft)
SIGINT	signals intelligence
SIM	Servizio Informazioni Militari (Italian Military Intelligence)
SISMI	Servizio per le Informazioni e la Sicurezza Militare (Military Intelligence and Security

	Service, Italy)
SS	Screw Steamer (prefix for civilian naval vessels)
Su	Sukhoi (the design bureau led by Pavel Ossipowich Sukhoi, also known as OKB-51)
SUCAP	Surface Combat Air Patrol
SyAAF	Syrian Arab Air Force
Technical	improvised fighting vehicle (typically an open-backed civilian 4WD modified to a gun truck)
TPS	Tactical Paint Scheme (USN)
USAF	United States Air Force
USN	United States Navy
USS	States Ship (prefix for US Navy's commissioned ships while in active commission)
USSR	Union of Soviet Socialist Republics (or Soviet Union)
VHF	very high frequency

ADDENDA/ERRATA:
LIBYAN AIR WARS PART 1, 1973–1985

Researching recent military history – especially in the case of such complex conflicts as those involving Libya in the 1970s and 1980s – is a never-ending task. It often happens that important information either arrives much too late for publishing in a specific volume, or must be omitted for reasons of space. In other cases, new or more detailed information appears from new sources precisely in reaction to a specific publication. The authors would therefore like to make the following amendments and corrections to that volume.

Chapter 2: Million-Man Army, p. 10

Further information regarding a huge Libyan order for a total of 110 Dassault Mirage 5 from December 1969 indicates that related negotiations actually began in 1968, while the country was still ruled by King Idris I. According to Bulhasen Saifelnasser's PhD-thesis 'Les relations franco-libyennes' (Thèse de Doctorat en Sciences Politiques, Université d'Auvergne-Clermont FD1) from 2008, p. 80, negotiations between Tripoli and France began in 1968, with Libyans expressing interest in 18 Mirage IIIs. When Muammar Muhammad Abu Minyar al-Gaddafi took over, these negotiations were actually restarted and Libyans expanded their order to 110 aircraft. The crucial reason for the French agreement to sell these aircraft was the cynical conclusion that the tiny Libyan Arab Air Force (LAAF) would take years to train enough pilots and ground personnel to operate all the Mirages, and their sale could thus not offset the balance of forces in the Middle East in the near term.

Chapter 2: Million-Man Army, p. 22–24

Additional information related to the short war between Egypt and Libya, fought in July 1977, emerged recently from declassified

reports of the French Air Force (Armée de l'Air, AdA), as follows:

- Egyptians have deployed four battalions (SAM-sites) of SA-2, four of SA-3s and SA-6s within the combat zone along the border with Libya.
- The Egyptian Air Force (EAF) raided the Gamal Abdel Nasser Air Base south of Tobruk (former RAF el-Adem) once on 22 July and three times on 23 July, causing heavy damage to ground installations. Among others, Egyptian bombs demolished a hangar where 11 SOCATA 235 Rallye training aircraft were stored, which were planned to be used for flying border patrols (Japanese company Sony was contracted to install video cameras on them).
- Overall, Egypt should have lost four Dassault Mirage 5s, four Sukhoi Su-7BMKs, two Mikoyan i Gurevich MiG-21s and two Tupolev Tu-16 bombers during this war (one of the Tu-16s should have been shot down by Libyan SA-3s, while another was shot down by cannon fire from a LAAF Mirage 5). Two EAF Su-7s returned to their bases in damaged condition.
- Libya should have lost eight Mirage 5s (one to fratricide fire, one to cannon fire from an Egyptian fighter, two in mid-air collision, one by accident and two damaged and written-off), five SOKO J-21 Jastrebs, 11 Rallyes and – possibly – two Mikoyan i Gurevich MiG-23s. Furthermore, two Mirages, four J-21 Jastrebs and one Aérospatiale SE.316B Alouette III helicopter were damaged, but repairable.[2]

Chapter 3: Chadian prequel, p. 32

Javier Nart, a Spanish journalist who has spent much of his career reporting from Chad and was a first-hand eyewitness to many of the developments described in this mini-series, has provided a host of additions and corrections for various details published in Volume 1. Among others, he corrected French claims according to which Chadian insurgents active in the Faya Largeau area in 1971 committed any atrocities against the local population. On the contrary, this was never the case, and for several good reasons: most of them came from the very same local population, which not only provided them with a support base but also a source of recruitment.

Chapter 4: Early Libyan Interventions, p. 35

According to Javier Nart, the attack on Faya in January 1978 was actually undertaken by the 2eme Armée du FROLINAT, reinforced by Acyl Ahmad's 2eme Armée Volcan and the symbolic support of the 1ére Armée-FPL, led by Mahammat Abba Sayd. Libyan support included a battery each of D30 howitzers (122mm calibre) and BM-21 multiple rocket launchers (MRLs) for artillery rockets (122mm calibre) of Soviet origin. Correspondingly, the Popular Armed Forces (Forces Armées Populaires, FAP) was established only after this battle, on 28 March 1978, through reorganisation of all the factions of FROLINAT and the Volcan Army.

Chapter 5: FON over Syrte, p. 41

Pit Weinert from Germany has provided a number of photographs from his collection, showing Italian authorities in the course of investigating the crash site of a Libyan Arab Air Force (LAAF) MiG-23MS flown by a Syrian Arab Air Force (SyAAF) pilot, named as 1st Lieutenant (1st Lt) Ezzedin Koal. As reported in Volume 1, an investigation by the LAAF concluded that Koal went into hypoxia due to a new oxygen mask that did not fit well enough. Set on 'semi auto-pilot', his MiG-23MS flew away and eventually crashed on Mount Sila in Calabria (southern Italy), after running out of fuel, on 18 July 1980.

Further to this issue, an exhaustive entry into the crash of this MiG-23 on Mount Sila posted on the Italian-language version of Wikiwand.com under the title 'Incidente aereo die Castelsilano' provided the following details about the aircraft and its pilot:

- The aircraft was a MiG-23MS, serial number 6950, powered by a Tumansky R-27-300 engine, made on 30 November 1976 and delivered to Libya on 27 August 1977. It was not armed with any missiles, carried no drop tanks and had no ammunition for internal cannon.[3]

- The pilot wore a black helmet with inscriptions in Cyrilic and the Arabic alphabet. The latter read 'EZZ-EIDN-KOAL' or 'EZZ-ETTN-KHAL'.[4]

- Libyan authorities identified the pilot as Captain Khalil Ezzeden, born in Benghazi on 17 March 1950. He obtained his military pilot licence in 1972, and by 1980 had flown SOKO G-2 Galebs, SOKO J-21 Jastrebs, MiG-21s and MiG-23s for a total of 927 hours in the course of training in the former Yugoslavia, Libya and Russia. He was certified as qualified for combat and pair leader. However, the Italian Military Intelligence and Security Service (Servizio per le Informazioni e la Sicurezza Militare, SISMI), concluded that

A pair of SOCATA 235 Rallye basic trainers at Malta in the early 1970s. Libya purchased 12 such aircraft from France. One defected to Egypt on 11 May 1977 with LAAF pilot Rahome Said el Asfar. The others were destroyed in the course of Egyptian air strikes against Gamal Abdel Nasser AB, on 22 and 23 July 1977. (Albert Grandolini Collection)

the pilot in question was Syrian of Palestinian origin, with the full name and rank of Captain Pilot Ezzedin Fadhil Khalil.[5]

- According to Libyans, the aircraft took off from Benina AB near Benghazi at 0945 local time on 18 July 1980, as a lead machine in a pair. Initially, it flew in direction of Marsa al-Burayqah (point A on the map below). Thirteen minutes into the flight, it turned in an eastern direction while climbing to an altitude of 9,500m (31,168ft), before turning east (point B) and climbing to an altitude of 10,000m (32,808ft). The MiG then continued climbing to 12,000m (39,370ft), and turned to a course of 330° (when reaching point C), instead of the expected 305°. Immediately afterwards, all contact with the pilot was lost. The wingman followed the flight lead until about 60km (37¼ miles) north of Benina. Left with only 1,400 litres (3,086.4lbs) of fuel in his tanks, he then decided to return to base. Khalil's MiG was last tracked by Libyan radars while flying along the same course about 300km (186½) north of Benina AB, still underway at an altitude of 12,000m. Libyan authorities launched a SAR operation in an area between 300 and 400km north of Benghazi, but found nothing.[6]

Khalil's body was returned to Libya with full military honours (at Italian expense; Libyans refused to pay for his transportation from Rome/Ciampino IAP to Tripoli), followed by the wreckage of his aircraft – minus ARK-15 radio compass, which was handed over to US intelligence services upon their explicit request (in turn causing some protests from Libya).[7]

Following an investigation, several Italian judges excluded any possibility of Khalil becoming involved in any kind of air combat, or even in any kind of interception of the Douglas DC-9 of Itavia that crashed into the Tyrrhenian Sea on 27 June 1980.

Chapter 5: FON over Syrte, pp. 44–51

Thirty-three years since the famous Syrte Gulf Incident of 19 August 1981, in which two Grumman F-14A Tomcat interceptors of US Navy (USN) squadron VF-41 'Black Aces' shot down two LAAF Sukhoi Su-22Ms, more details of the Libyan version of the clash became available.

According to the blog by one of the relatives of the involved

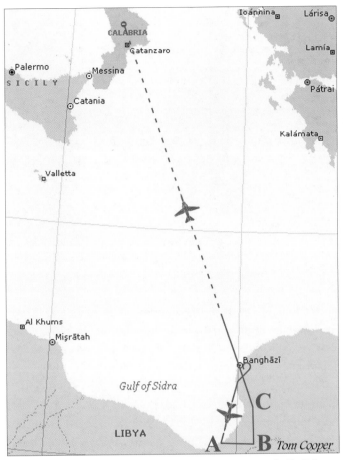

Map with reconstruction of the last flight of Captain Ezzedin Fadhil Khalil, on 18 July 1980, according to official Libyan data. (Map by Tom Cooper)

Wreckage of Ezzedin Koal's MiG-23MS next to that of the Itavia DC-9. Of interest is that, although certainly not related to the tragic demise of a Douglas DC-9 of Itavia Airlines over the Tyrrhenian Sea, on 27 June 1980, some wreckage of Koal's MiG-23MS was brought to the same hangar where Italian and foreign investigators reconstructed the wreckage of the airliner. (Pit Weinert Collection)

Still from a video showing the fin section of Ezzedin Koal's MiG-23MS, together with Libyan national markings and serial number 6950. (Pit Weinert Collection)

Libyan inspectors studying wreckage of Ezzedin Koal's MiG-23MS at Mount Sila. Note the frame for the MiG's windshield. (Pit Weinert Collection)

Libyan pilots, the two Su-22Ms were from No. 1022 Squadron LAAF, based at Ghurdabiya AB, outside Syrte – a unit then under the command of Major Abdelsalam Djalloud. Commander of Ghurdabiyah AB was Colonel Dumuha Ramadhan Zaid.

The account of air combat between Tomcats and Sukhois is rather short. Libyan radars should have detected eight F-14s early that morning, of which two crossed the 'Line of Death' and thus – from the Libyan point of view – violated sovereign Libyan airspace over the Gulf of Syrte. Two Su-22s were scrambled from Ghurdabyiah AB in response, piloted by Captain Belkacem Emsik al-Zintani, and 1st Lieutenant Mokhtar el-Arabi al-Jaafari. The

Sukhois climbed to an altitude of 7,000m (22,936ft) and received the order to 'shoot down the intruders'.

As the two formations approached, al-Zintani saw two F-14s making a 180° turn – while still well in front of him – as soon as they saw the Libyan fighters. Knowing his Su-22 could not turn with Tomcats, al-Zintani made a right turn and what he only described as a 'surprise manoeuvre' – which should have brought him into a position directly behind one of the Tomcats. Moments later he fired a missile and 'destroyed' the F-14, supposedly killing its pilot, Commander Henry Kleeman. This account seemingly ignores the fact that the F-14A Tomcat was a two-seater, and does not mention the supposed fate of Lieutenant Dave Venlet, Kleeman's radar intercept officer, with even a single word.

'Evidence' for al-Zintani's claim was provided in the form of a piece of wreckage found by local fishermen several days later: because the LAAF concluded this was a piece of Kleeman's Tomcat, al-Zintani was subsequently credited with a confirmed kill and the wreckage in question put on display in No. 1022 Squadron's ready room.

Immediately afterwards, the two Sukhois came under attack from six other Tomcats and both were shot down. Al-Zintani and al-Jaafari ejected about 75km off the coast of Syrte, and al-Zintani saw one F-14 'circling' above him until he touched the water.

This account indicates that the situational awareness of al-

Group photo of pilots serving with No. 1022 Squadron LAAF in summer 1981, in front of one of the Su-22s (or Su-22M-2Ks) they flew at the time. (via Pit Weinert)

FAZA Major M'Bo in front of a table listing all Zairian aircraft deployed in Chad in 1983. (Pascal Mikine)

Zintani and al-Jaafari was quite poor, while some parts of this narrative appear fabricated to 'fit' the legend. Namely, while Kleeman did make a near 180° turn 'in front' of two Sukhois, he did so only about 150m above and 300m in front of the Libyans. Because of the speed and relative positions of all the involved aircraft, there was no way that al-Zintani could put his Sukhoi behind the lead Tomcat – and certainly no 'surprise manoeuvre'. On the contrary, because the Sukhois could not turn hard enough, they ended in front of Kleeman, with the USN formation leader subsequently going after al-Jaafari's Su-22M. Zintani didn't fire 'by accident': he opened fire at the F-14 he saw approaching him from above (Kleeman's aircraft), without waiting for his R-13M missile to obtain a lock-on necessary to track its target. Even if the missile did obtain a lock-on – which is unlikely, considering the R-13M could not do so from the aspect from which al-Zintani had fired – it could not physically track a target moving perpendicular at that range and such a rate of closure, because this would be outside the limits of its seeker-head.[8]

Finally, al-Zintani's account also reveals that he actually never saw the second F-14, flown by Muczynski, who shot him down. Although rather cryptic in this regards, his account indicates that he was subsequently attacked by 'six Tomcats' and shot down. Surprisingly, while providing extensive details about his ejection, parachuting into the sea and hours of swimming while waiting for search and rescue (SAR) helicopter to find him, al-Zintani didn't mention the fate of his wingman at all. As far as is known, al-Jaafari survived his downing and was also safely recovered.

Another interesting detail form this account is the narrative about a subsequent discussion between a person named only as 'X' and Gaddafi. According to this account, the Libyan leader was quite angered by the loss of two Su-22Ms and asked 'X' why they sent two rather 'unsuitable' fighter-bombers to intercept the F-14s. Djalloud came to the help of 'X', explaining that Ghurdabiyah was the nearest air base and that it had only Su-22s available at the time.

This might indicate that despite US warnings prior of the FON exercise in the Gulf of Syrte, the appearance of two F-14s south of the 'Line of Death' on the morning of 19 August 1981 took the LAAF by surprise. This in turn resulted in a situation where Libyan commanders failed to take necessary precautions and deploy interceptor aircraft at this important air base.

Chapter 6: Showdown in Chad, p. 53

According to Javier Nat, the LAAF never repaired and lengthened the runway at Faya Largeau. On the contrary, this was only hardened – but not asphalted – in 1990, and could support only the operation of lighter, propeller-powered aircraft during the 1980s.

Chapter 6: Showdown in Chad, p. 55

A reader who prefers to remain anonymous has provided us with a scan of article 'Pilote de Chasse au Tchad', published by Francois Soudan in *Jeune Afrique* magazine in December 1983. The feature in question was primarily dedicated to operations of three Dassault Mirage 5M fighter-bombers deployed by the Zairian Air Force (Force Aérienne Zaïroise, FAZA) in Chad, in 1983. As well as providing details about the landing accident of the Mirage 5M with serial number 402 (while flown by Captain Mpele Mpele), the article further cited a supposed involvement of FAZA fighter-bombers in fighting for Abéche. However, according to information provided by various French Air Force (Armée de l'Air, AdA) pilots present in Chad at the time, Abéche was too far away for Zairian Mirages that were based at N'Djamena International Airport, and they never flew a single combat sortie over the area.

One of the photographs taken by photographer Pascal Mikine and used to illustrate that article reveals interesting additional details about Zairian aircraft deployed in Chad that year. These included Mirage 5Ms with serial numbers 402, 404 and 412, Aermacchi MB.326s with serial numbers FG477, FG479 and FG482, and an Aerospatiale SA.330 Puma with registration 9T-HP19.

Chapter 6: Showdown in Chad, pp. 55–56, 61

In the course of research for Parts 2 and 3 of this mini-series, authors have found the following additional information related

Handcuffed and with bare feet, Major Abdel-Salam Muhammed Shafraddine was presented to the Chadian and international public in early August 1983. He was shot down by a FIM-43A Redeye MANPAD operated by a group of French mercenaries near Faya Largeau, while flying a Su-22 fighter-bomber. (Albert Grandolini Collection)

to the first loss of a LAAF Sukhoi Su-22 fighter-bomber over Chad, on 4 August 1983. According to Ahmad Allam-Mi's book *Tchad en Guerre: Tractations politiques et diplomatiques, 1975–1990* (Paris, l'Harmattan, 2014, pp.160–161), Chad and United States of America signed a Mutual Defence Assistance Agreement in July 1983. In accordance with that agreement, Washington provided a batch of FIM-43A Redeye man-portable air defence systems (MANPADs) to N'Djamena, which arrived together with three

US Army specialists. However, instead of training Chadians, the Americans issued Redeyes to a group of 30 French operatives of the French Military Intelligence under the command of Colonel Roger Grillot. This group was further reinforced by a team of mercenaries recruited by Bob Denard and led by René Dulac. This team deployed to Faya Largeau in early August 1983, and its first kill was the LAAF Su-22.

According to an article published in the *New York Times* on 9 August 1983, the downed pilot was Major Abdel-Salam Muhammed Shafraddine, who was 43 years old at the time. Shafraddine, who had received training in Libya and the Union of Soviet Socialist Republics (USSR, Soviet Union) ejected safely and was captured by troops of Hissène Habré's National Armed Forces of Chad (Forces Armées Nationales Tchadiennes, FANT). He was brought to N'Djamena and presented to the international press a few days later. In the course of an interview that lasted about 45 minutes, Shafraddine explained that he was assigned to a squadron equipped with 12 Su-22s, which had flown between 40 and 50 air strikes against targets in the Faya Largeau area during the five days preceding his capture. They usually operated in flights of two aircraft armed with 250kg and 500kg calibre general purpose bombs and napalm canisters. He added that the squadron was visited by Gaddafi a few days before the attack on Faya-Largeau began, and that he heard radio-messages from crews of Tupolev Tu-22 bombers engaged in attacks in the same area.

CHAPTER 1
LIBYAN AIR FORCE IN THE EARLY 1980s

The area that is nowadays within the borders of Libya saw some of the first applications of air power in the history of warfare. In November 1911, Italian military pilot Lieutenant Giulio Gavotti flew the first mass-produced military aircraft ever during the Italian invasion of what were then Tripolitania and Cyrenaica, to attack Turkish military positions. For three years of the Second World War, between 1940 and 1943, Great Britain and Italy – subsequently joined by Germany – fought a series of bitter battles for domination over Libya and Egypt. All three parties deployed large contingents of their air forces in support of ground- and naval operations, and towards the end of this campaign, US air power also began appearing in this theatre of operations.

Subsequently administered by the British as a UN trusteeship, Libya was released into independence in January 1952. Nevertheless, Great Britain and the USA retained two large air bases in the country until 1970: Wheelus Air Force Base in Tripoli and el-Adem Air Base south of Tobruq. These included lengthy deployments of nuclear-armed fighter-bombers, such as F-100 Super Sabres of the US Air Force (USAF). A small Royal Libyan Air Force was established under some US pressure in 1962, but this had only a slow development.

The situation changed dramatically following a military coup that brought Gaddafi to power in Libya in September 1969. The first 10 years of his rule over the country can only be described as an extremely turbulent period. After nationalising the oil industry and imposing a number of far-reaching reforms of administrative and constitutional nature domestically, Gaddafi began increasing the prices of Libyan oil. This resulted in an outright explosion of national income, reaching levels where Tripoli proved unable to spend its income – despite a subsequent decline in oil prices and several times doubling investment allocations to its development planning. While there was no lack of financing for grandiose schemes related to agricultural development, communications, housing, education and heavy industry, Libya lacked the human resources to carry them out. It would take an entire generation for the situation to improve to any degree.

On the international scene, Gaddafi initially pursued the concept of establishing a super-state uniting all Arab countries. While welcomed by many other Arab and African statesmen, this idea proved fruitless. On the contrary, for a country declared as fiercely dedicated to the principle of Arab unity, Libya found it remarkably difficult to get along with most of its neighbours.

After Gaddafi openly criticised the 'limited objectives' of Egypt during the October 1973 war with Israel, his relationship with Egypt deteriorated markedly during the mid-1970s. A long-simmering feud culminated in a short war, in July 1977, during which the inexperienced Libyan military suffered heavy losses. Relations between Cairo and Tripoli remained stormy and eventually collapsed after Egyptian President Anwar el-Sadat made peace with Israel in 1979 while failing to reach a negotiated settlement over the issues of Palestinian autonomy or the West Bank of Jordan. Gaddafi denounced Sadat's 'betrayal of Arabs' and played a crucial role in imposing the boycott of Egypt by nearly all members of the Arab League. The Libyan leader not only called for the 'execution' of Sadat, but publicly cheered when the Egyptian president was assassinated in 1981, setting alarm bells ringing everywhere between Washington and Khartoum. Although officially declaring a union with Sudan, because of developments in Egypt and Chad, Libya subsequently found itself in confrontation with that country too.

On its western borders, Libya began provoking problems with Tunisia. While signing an agreement in 1974 to merge their country with Libya into a joint 'Islamic Arab Republic', the Tunisians had changed their mind, and relations with Tripoli remained strained well into the 1980s, not helped by a long-standing dispute over oil exploration rights in the Gulf of Gabes.

When his diplomacy failed, Gaddafi began supporting radical movements – first around the Middle East and Africa, and later even in Europe. After accusing the Palestinian Liberation Organisation (PLO) of moving towards accommodation with Israel and 'selling the Palestinians short', Gaddafi closed its offices in Libya and established ties to other Palestinian militant groups instead, providing them with arms, training and financing in 1979 and 1980. Unsurprisingly, this only worsened relations between Libya and several Western powers, already sour since 1973, when Tripoli declared the Gulf of Syrte (known as the Gulf of Sidra in the USA) in the central Mediterranean 'an indivisible part' of Libyan sovereign territorial waters. In accordance with that claim, LAAF interceptors regularly attacked and opened fire on aircraft and ships wearing US, French and Italian flags.

Gaddafi's followers acted aggressively against Western diplomats and representatives in Libya too. In December 1979, Libyan demonstrators chanting pro-Iranian slogans stormed and burned part of the US embassy in Tripoli, and in February 1980, demonstrators sacked the French embassy in Tripoli and consulate in Benghazi. After Great Britain expelled several Libyan diplomats, the British embassy in Tripoli was fire-bombed in June 1980.

During the same year, Gaddafi announced Libya's union with Syria. Although Syrian President Hafez al-Assad immediately accepted and signed a 14-point proclamation announcing that the two had become a 'single state', this union proved to be a short-lived affair of only symbolic nature, but subsequently cooperation between Damascus and Tripoli was intensified to unprecedented levels. Indeed, after Libya became the first Arab state to openly side with non-Arab Iran when it was invaded by Iraq in 1980, Syria followed in fashion, and both countries began supporting Tehran through arms deliveries.

Meanwhile, continuous social and political experimentation by Gaddafi – including severe curtailing of entrepreneurial opportunities in the private sector – hit the Libyan economy hard during the early 1980s, and was seen with increasing distaste and apprehension by many segments of Libyan society. Tripoli reacted fiercely to any dissent: in 1980, it ordered thousands of exiled dissidents to return to Libya or be 'liquidated'. When these refused to do so, Gaddafi began deploying hit squads to intimidate and assassinate opponents living in exile in Great Britain and the USA in 1979 and 1980.

Preoccupied with other affairs, the administration of US President Jimmy Carter failed to counter Libyan claims and the provocative behaviour of the Libyan military, but the situation changed dramatically once Ronald Reagan was elected into the White House in early 1981. Reagan recognised Libya as a 'genuine threat' to US interests in the Middle East and Africa, accused it of supporting up to 30 different terrorist organisations world-wide and of deploying intelligence operatives and agents to assassinate Libyan oppositionals in the USA. In summer 1981, the US Navy received the order to deploy two carrier battle groups into the central Mediterranean and run a 'freedom of navigation' (FON) exercise over the Gulf of Syrte. During the second day of this exercise, on 19 August 1981, two Sukhoi Su-22Ms of the LAAF attacked two Grumman F-14A Tomcats of the US Navy flying over the Gulf of Syrte and opened fire. In return, the USN fighters shot down both Libyan fighter jets.

Subsequently, Reagan's administration began not only developing further plans to confront the Libyan claim for the Gulf of Syrte, but also to undermine Gaddafi's domestic power base, tarnish Libya's image and position abroad and decrease its influence in the Middle East and Africa. It was very much due to US interest that Chad – Libya's southern neighbour – subsequently developed into a major battlefield between Gaddafi's government, the USA and France.

Meanwhile – and remarkably for an outspokenly anti-Communist state – Libya established ties with the Soviet Union and reached an arms agreement with Moscow in May 1974. This resulted in one of biggest arms deals in the history of the Middle East until that time, including deliveries of nearly 400 combat aircraft to the LAAF. However, unknown to the public, Libyan-Soviet relations subsequently experienced a period of tensions too – primarily because of Libyan dissatisfaction over the quality and capabilities of Soviet-manufactured armaments, but also over the quality of training provided to Libyan personnel in the USSR and at home. Nevertheless, in the USA and Western Europe, Libya was seen as a 'Soviet client' and thus a threat to NATO's southern flank by 1980, and relations with Tripoli became tense.

It was against this backdrop that tensions between the USA and Libya in particular, but also between France and Libya, reached their highest point in 1985 and 1986, and resulted in what was de-facto an undeclared war.-

During tensions between Libya and Tunisia, in early 1980, the small Tunisian Air Force was forced to deploy some of its Aermacchi MB.326s of the Escadrille 11 to Djerba Airport, close to Libyan border. Subsequently, Tunisian Air Force was bolstered through purchases of Northrop F-5E/F Tiger II. (Albert Grandolini Collection)

For nearly 40 years fate of Libya and its armed forces was closely tied to that of Muammar al-Gaddafi. This photograph of 'Brother Leader' came into being during one of military parades in Tripoli, in late 1970s. (Albert Grandolini Collection)

LAAF in the early 1980s

The 1970s saw an explosive expansion of the Libyan Arab Air Force. In less than 10 years, this small and underdeveloped branch totalling about 400 officers and other ranks in 1969, was expanded through the acquisition of 110 Dassault Mirage 5D/5DE/5DR and 5DD fighter-bombers, 64 MiG-21bis/UMs, 54 MiG-23MS/UBs, 35 MiG-23BNs, 60 MiG-25P/RB/Pus, 36 Su-22/22Ms, 38 Mirage F.1AD/ED and Bs, 12 Tupolev Tu-22 bombers, 50 transport aircraft, nearly 400 different training aircraft and over 100 helicopters.

The LAAF not only lacked pilots and ground personnel to operate even half of this equipment, but also the support infrastructure necessary for its maintenance. About a dozen new air bases were constructed around the country, followed by two dozen civilian airfields with a secondary military role. Libya also invested massively in the training of new personnel. Lacking necessary facilities at home, large groups of cadets underwent basic training in Yugoslavia until an Air Force Academy was constructed at Misurata AB. However, advanced and combat training remained a source of massive problems – not only for the LAAF, but the entire Libyan military. Help provided by French and Pakistani instructors in training Libyans to fly Mirages proved insufficient,

while the quality of training provided to Libyan pilots in the USSR was below expectations. Because of the huge demand for new pilots, so many cadets were sent for further training to different countries abroad that by 1980 the LAAF pilots were flying in several different languages: those trained in France used French, those trained in Pakistan and similar countries used English, and those trained in Eastern Europe used the Russian language. Unsurprisingly, Libyans began searching for an alternative that would offer a solution for this and many other problems.

American Renegades

Successive commanders of the Libyan Arab Air Force attempted to solve the problem of lack of personnel in several ways. To begin with, they invited friendly air forces – foremost those of Egypt, but also France and Pakistan – to detach groups of their officers and other ranks to Libya. Through the mid-1970s, a solution was sought through the hiring of mercenaries. It was in this fashion that Tripoli established particularly close ties in 1976 to two former employees of the Central Intelligence Agency (CIA): Frank E. Tespil and Edwin P Wilson.

Originally, Tespil and Wilson ran an arms-dealing business – OSI-SA Import-Export Co. – based in Great Britain. Essentially, they did the same as many other expatriates at the time, as related British laws and regulations were still relatively lax. Not long after they established links to Tripoli and sold it a relatively small shipment of night-vision goggles and C-4 explosives, the Libyans prompted the Americans to start hiring instructors who could train operatives of the Libyan military intelligence in assassinations of Libyan dissidents abroad.[9] This aspect of cooperation between Gaddafi and the two Americans was further expanded when Tespil and Wilson were contracted to provide pilots and ground personnel who could serve with the LAAF. Run via a Swiss-based company, SCFMO, this enterprise resulted in the deployment of between 150 and 200 American and British citizens in Libya between 1977 and 1981, and the establishment of a paramilitary company named Jamahirya Air Transport.

Pilots and ground personnel hired by SCFMO were largely Americans, but also people like British pilot John Anthony Stubbs, known to have flown Lockheed C-130H Hercules transports (also during operations in Chad) and several Frenchmen. Two other pilots hired by SCFMO were Americans who test-flew MiG-23s and helped Libyans write a flying manual of the type that enabled the LAAF to properly train its pilots.[10]

However, regardless how successful, cooperation between the

In the late 1970s and early 1980s, the LAAF's C-130-related operations were heavily dependent on hired mercenary pilots from the USA and Great Britain. This photograph of the C-130H serial number 111 was taken a few years later. (Marinus Dirk Tabak)

Libyan authorities, Tespil and Wilson could never grant the level of support the LAAF needed in order to become an effective military force. Realising this quite early, Libya soon began searching for a much more powerful source of advice and instruction, and they found it in a way very few foreign observers of relevant developments in the early 1970s could ever expect.

Operation L: Czechoslovak Connection

When Gaddafi took power in 1969, his anti-communist rhetoric was resented by the Soviet Union and her Warsaw Pact allies. Nevertheless, concluding that the communist-ruled countries of Eastern Europe were capable of offering large amounts of relatively simple arms at cheaper prices and shorter delivery terms, and that their deliveries were usually linked to fewer political conditions than those from the West, Libya began establishing ties to several of the governments in question. As so often in the troublesome history of relations between different Arab states with strong anti-communist politics and nations of the Warsaw Pact, it was Czechoslovakia that made the first step.

While Prague considered Gaddafi a 'reactionary', income in hard currency was most welcome for the Czechoslovak economy.[11] Thus it was not long before representatives from Tripoli found an agreement with representatives from Prague and the first contract – including an order for 154 Czechoslovak-manufactured T-55 main battle tanks (MBTs) and 100 OT-62 armoured personnel carriers (APCs), infantry weapons, ammunition and spare parts – was signed in early 1970.[12]

Aiming to become self-sufficient in production of heavy armament, the Libyans entered negotiations with Czechoslovakia in 1972 for the acquisition of entire factories for production of heavy armament and facilities for the refurbishment of armoured vehicles. Following protracted talks, Prague turned down all such requests in 1974, by when it was obvious that Tripoli lacked not only the industrial capacity and skilled workforce, but also management capabilities for such projects, and because there was no licence agreement with the USSR that would authorise

Czechoslovakia to sell arms of Soviet design to third parties.

Meanwhile, and especially after the October 1973 Arab-Israeli War, Tripoli began pushing Czechoslovaks by placing additional arms orders. Following intense and thorough negotiations in Prague between 11 and 14 February 1974, Libya issued an order for 480 additional T-55 MBTs and 210 T-55K (command variant), related spares and ammunition. Additional contracts signed during following years eventually added a further 1,065 T-55s to this order, and the construction of tank-crew training facilities. Knowing that extensions of Libyan orders were surpassing the capabilities of the Libyan military to acquire the equipment in question and train its own personnel, Czechoslovaks agreed to provide their own instructors. These were initially to serve in a training camp for tank crews. Learning about the quality of training provided by Prague, the LAAF soon requested Czechoslovaks to provide a much larger contingent of instructors from their air force. Thus began what Prague ran under the code name 'Operation L'.

The first group of Czechoslovak Air Force instructors arrived in Libya during the second half of 1977 and was commanded by Major-General Juraj Lalo. Initially based at the former Wheelus AB – renamed as Umm Aittitiqah but colloquially known as 'Mitiga' – this group moved to Ghurdabiyah AB, outside Syrte, later the same year. This facility was still incomplete and it took the Czechoslovaks several months of very hard work under Spartan conditions to establish the 2nd Air School there. The purpose of this institution was to provide basic and advanced tactical training for LAAF cadets who already received basic flight training elsewhere. In this fashion, Czechoslovaks were to help bring the training of all new Libyan combat pilots and instructors to the same standard. During 1978, the original group of instructors was expanded to 360: the additional personnel helped establish the 1st Air Staff School at Mitiga AB. By the end of the same year, no less than 1,093 Libyan cadets – including not only pilots but ground personnel too – were attending courses at the 2nd Air School.[13]

Albatross Orders

In the meantime, tensions between Egypt and Libya resulted in a short war, and Tripoli requested Prague to stop delivering arms and spares to Cairo, offering additional – highly lucrative – contracts as compensation. Curious to safeguard large-scale orders from Libya, Prague complied, despite immense pressure from Moscow, which was still keen to safeguard its relations with Egypt. One of

Libyan interest in Soviet-designed T-55 tanks of Czechoslovak production (as seen here) led to the establishment of intensive military cooperation between Prague and Tripoli. (Tom Cooper Collection)

During the 1980s, Libya placed such massive orders in Czechoslovakia that much of the output of local industry was sold out for years in advance. This is one of the Czechoslovak-manufactured T-72 main-battle tanks in Libyan service. (Tom Cooper collection)

the most obvious compensation contracts with Libya became the LAAF order for Aero L-39ZO Albatross jet trainers.

Negotiations between Prague and Tripoli relating to the acquisition of L-39s began in April 1977. A Libyan delegation that visited Czechoslovakia requested delivery of 64 aircraft and aid in setting-up a flying school capable of training between 300 and 400 cadets in a three-year curriculum. Around the same time, Tripoli attempted to place additional huge orders with Prague for its army, including 80 BM-21 multiple-rocket launchers (MRLs), 50 MT-55 bridge-laying tanks, 50 T-55ARV armoured engineer vehicles, 240 T-813 Kolos heavy trucks and a factory for the production of infantry weapons. While Moscow – now curious to safeguard its own contracts with Libya – prevented realisation of most of the army-related deals, the Libyans did manage to convince the Czechoslovaks to deliver L-39s. The first contract resulted in the delivery of 72 L-39ZOs in 1977 and 1978.

In 1979, the Commander-in-Chief (C-in-C) of the Czechoslovak Air Force, General Josef Remek, visited Libya and inspected the work of his instructors in situ. His negotiations with top LAAF officers and representatives of the Libyan Ministry of Defence eventually led to the second Libyan order for L-39s, 48 of which were delivered in 1979 and 1980. Around the same time, the Czechoslovak military mission to Libya was expanded to about 600, including 98 pilots. Additional personnel enabled the establishment of the 3rd Air School, based at Mitiga AB, and an agreement for the training of 480 Libyan pilots and 1,120 ground personnel of the LAAF in Libya through the period 1980–1983. One hundred Libyan officers also underwent specialised training at various higher educational facilities in Czechoslovakia.

Between 1977 and 1981, Czechoslovak Air Force personnel in Libya trained no less than 1,100 Libyans as pilots and ground personnel in projects worth about US$100 million. For this purpose, they used 72 L-39s from the first batch and a few TL-39 simulators operated by three air schools. By that time,

the 2nd Air School was organised in no less than five training squadrons (Czechoslovaks called these 'regiments'), each of which was staffed by 10 instructors, each of whom was responsible for three Libyan cadets. Each such unit was dual-commanded, with a Czechoslovak officer in charge of training and technical procedures, while a Libyan officer was responsible for all other issues, including discipline.[14]

On 1 September 1980, a special graduation ceremony was held at the 2nd Air School in Ghurdabya, when 113 Libyan pilots, 384 mechanics and 13 flight controllers graduated. At the time, 360 additional pilots and more than 1,000 technicians were still undergoing training: after some dropped out, 284 pilots and 873 technicians graduated in 1981.

Still in need of more pilots, Tripoli further intensified its cooperation with Prague through orders for the third – and final – batch of 60 L-39s, all of which were delivered in 1981, and for 19 Aero L-410 Turbolet light transports, which arrived in Libya by 1983 (for a summary of L-39-deliveries to Libya, see Table 1).

Some of the additional L-39s were necessary to replace unavoidable attrition caused by various training incidents. Some of these were fatal: five Czechoslovak instructors are known to have been killed during their tours of duty in Libya in the 1970s and 1980s. Other aircraft were necessary because Czechoslovak-run air schools of the LAAF also trained pilots from Ghana, Nigeria, Uganda and even some from West Sahara.

Table 1: Deliveries of L-39s to Libya

Variant	Number of aircraft delivered	Year
L-39ZO	72	1977–1978
L-39ZO	48	1979–1980
L-39ZO	60	1981
Totals	180	

One of 180 L-39ZOs delivered to Libya in the period 1977–1981 was this example, serialled 8215. Notable is the patch of one of the flying schools run by Czechoslovak Air Force personnel in Libya, applied below the cockpit, and original camouflage pattern (applied before delivery) consisting of beige and two shades of green. (Jean-Marie Lipka)

A group of LAAF L-39ZOs with Libyan students in front and Czechoslovak instructors in rear cockpits, in the early 1980s. (Vaclav Havner via Albert Grandolini)

Czechoslovak Experiences

Except for rather primitive working and housing conditions early on, the only major problem experienced by Czechoslovaks during their work in Libya was language. Because only a handful of them spoke Arabic, and no Libyans spoke any of the East European languages, but most at least understood English, the latter became the working language. The majority of Libyan cadets trained by Czechoslovaks received their basic flight training from Italians and Yugoslavs in that language. It appears that this solution was quite effective, as not only were the Czechoslovaks very satisfied and proud about their work, but the LAAF was happy with their services too. Many LAAF cadets who pressed on with their training proved to be competent pilots.

The success of the Czechoslovak training mission eventually reached a level where the LAAF requested more of its pilots and officers to be accepted for advanced training on fast jets (such as MiG-21s and MiG-23s) in Czechoslovakia. Starting in February 1980, corresponding courses were provided by the Czechoslovak Air Force Academy 'Slovak National Uprising' at Kosice. However, while it is known that 40 LAAF pilots underwent training on MiG-21s there, it remains unclear whether other plans were ever realised. It seems that even the acquisition of five additional MiG-21UM two-seat conversion trainers for them was called off amid some resistance from the Soviets.[15]

One of the Czechoslovak instructor pilots in Libya was Major Jaromir Smekal. Initially posted to Mitiga AB in 1979, his team was temporarily redeployed to the newly-constructed Ukba Ibn an-Nafi AB (also known as el-Woutia), close to the Tunisian border, before finally settling down at Ghurdabiyah AB in March 1980, when the 2nd Air School became operational. Smekal flew a total of 889.17 hours in 1,655 sorties during the four years of his tour of duty in Libya. These included 222 flight hours over the sea and 1,614 sorties with Libyan cadets.

Another Czechoslovak instructor in Libya was Major Vaclav Havner, who joined the 2nd Air School in September 1983, when the team of instructors at Ghurdabiyah AB was led by Colonel Jaroslav Sramek. Havner recalled that by that time postings to Libya were much sought after, because many of the several hundred Czechoslovaks who served in Libya – including a number of pilots discharged from service at home due to their age, and others who worked for the national airline CSA – came back home as 'rich men'. One of the reasons was that the Libyans proved ready to pay for almost everything without enquiring about the cost. For example, much of the equipment delivered to Libya was described as 'brand new', although it was actually second-hand, and only overhauled before delivery. This was particularly the case with tractors used to tow aircraft at several air bases – all of which were driven by Czechoslovak civilians who were receiving a 'very interesting' salary for their services. Havner further recalled that the usual flight schedule included four flying hours a day, with an average of more than 250 hours per year for every instructor – several times more than that accumulated by an average Czechoslovak pilot at home.[16]

Havner recalled that the Libyans imposed not only stringent security measures but also showed unusual suspicion towards all foreigners: they were strictly segregated by their nationality and no contact was permitted, even between Czechoslovaks and Soviets. It seems that Tripoli had good reasons for such measures: Czechoslovak military intelligence is known to have developed a network of agents and informers within the Libyan military, led by the Military Attaché to the embassy in Tripoli, Colonel Frantisek Sykora. The primary task of Sykora's informants was actually to monitor and evaluate US and NATO intentions regarding Libya and other Arab countries around the Middle East, but also to evaluate Western military equipment acquired by Libya and other foreign 'liberation organisations' based in the country. Sykora's agents were especially curious to obtain any documentation about air combat tactics taught to Libyans by their Western instructors.[17]

Best Times

Cooperation between Czechoslovakia and Libya reached its zenith in the period 1980–1983, by when 618 Czechoslovak instructors were in the country while the worth of related contracts reached US$480 million. The number of Czechoslovak personnel increased to 925 when the 3rd Air School became operational at Ukba Ibn an-Nafi AB in 1980, and the Libyans began developing plans for the establishment of another such facility, intended to train between 90 and 120 pilots and between 240 and 280 technicians a year.

However, subsequent developments spoiled much Libyan planning and many Czechoslovak hopes. Not only were a number of new contracts never signed, but the pace of deliveries gradually decreased. Even the further development of the 3rd Air School began lagging behind schedule. The primary reasons were several Soviet interventions: Moscow had its own agenda related to the sale of armament to Libya, and always strongly resisted any possible agreements related to licence production rights. Furthermore, Libyans not only proved unable to provide the required number of cadets, but began to experience economic difficulties because of a drop in oil prices and US embargoes imposed in 1981.

Expecting to be paid in cash, Prague felt forced to refuse extensions of different loans provided to Tripoli. Simultaneously, Prague had to cancel a number of Libyan orders because the extension of orders from Tripoli began to delay deliveries of modern armament to the Czechoslovak military, as the local industry could simply not satisfy both demands.

Several attempts to improve the situation led to a number of meetings between top officials from both sides, and some last large orders. For example, in March 1980, the Deputy Minister for Foreign Trade of Czechoslovak Republic, Frantisek Langer, visited Tripoli to sign a contract for 600 BMP-1 infantry fighting vehicles (IFVs), worth US$172 million, delivered between 1981 and 1983. Similarly, the CinC Libyan Armed Forces, Brigadier-General Abu Bakr Younis Jaber, visited Prague in 1980, prompting negotiations that resulted in contracts for the delivery of overhaul facilities for BMP-1s and L-39s, 80 152mm calibre Dana self-propelled howitzers (SPHs), 100,000 122mm calibre artillery rockets and the modernisation of T-55 MBTs delivered in the 1970s.[18]

Another visit by Brigadier General Jaber to Prague, followed

A group of Czechoslovak instructors with a Libyan L-39ZO in Libya. They were instrumental in training several hundreds of new LAAF fighter-pilots between 1979 and 1986.
(Vaclav Havner via Albert Grandolini)

A study of a LAAF L-39ZO armed with a pair of UB-16-57 pods for 57mm calibreunguided rocket pods, during one of thousands of training sorties run under the supervision of Czechoslovak instructors. (Vaclav Havner via Albert Grandolini)

by a visit by Gaddafi himself in 1983, brought to light Libyan dissatisfaction over repeated delays in deliveries of Czechoslovak arms. As well as discussing the postponed delivery of 100,000 BM-21 rockets, the Libyan leader went on to request no less than 4,000 Czechoslovak-manufactured T-72 MBTs and 1,000 BMP-1s, together with several facilities for maintenance of heavy military equipment. Explaining that Czechoslovak industry could not deliver more than 120 MBTs a year, and arguing with Soviet refusals to provide licence rights, Prague agreed to deliver 600 T-72s and 300 BMP-1s between 1982 and 1992. Even then, this Libyan order prevented a similar deal with Syria and forced the Czechoslovak People's Army to release 200 of its own T-72s for delivery to Libya. Furthermore, out of 1,600 BM-1s ordered by Libya, only a total of 666 were delivered by 1989. This was to prove the last major Libyan order for Czechoslovak arms.

In 1983 and 1984, the Libyans revised their military requirements. Apparently giving up several large-scale development projects, the LAAF abandoned the idea of setting up a third flight school (planned for Brach AB), and instead opened a small training centre for L-410 transports at Misurata AB. When Czechoslovakia proved unable or unwilling to provide such services, Poland was contracted with the delivery and construction of an overhaul facility for Mil Mi-2 helicopters and the provision of necessary instructors for that work.

Prague then began a gradual process of disengagement from Libya. Although the number of Czechoslovak instructors in the country reached no less than 1,218 in 1984 (770 of these were assigned to the LAAF), necessitating the appointment of Major General Zdenek Kac as commander of the contingent, the best times of Czechoslovak-Libyan cooperation were over. Although still verbally supporting Gaddafi, and the last of its instructors only leaving Libya in 1990, Czechoslovakia minimised its involvement in the country from 1986.

Ignoring Problems: Italian Connection

Along with Czechoslovaks, Italians played a very important role in the further development of the LAAF during the late 1970s and early 1980s. As described in Part 1 of this mini-series, Libya came into being within its modern-day borders during Italian invasion and occupation, which began in 1911. Many Italian colonists remained in the country after the end of the Second World War, but nearly all were expelled when Muammar Muhammad Abu Minyar al-Gaddafi came to power in 1969–1970.

The delivery of Mirage 5s by France and Gaddafi's verbal threats prompted the Italians to reinforce their air defence assets on Sicily. In the course of Operation Mare Caldo (Hot Sea) in 1972, North American F-86K Sabres of the XII Gruppo (12th Squadron) of the 51st Stormo (Wing) were deployed to Catania-Sigonella AB, while Lockheed F-104G Starfighters of the CLIV Gruppo (154th Squadron), 6th Stormo deployed to Trapani-Birgi AB. Immediately upon arrival, the Starfighters flew a series of 'showing the flag' sorties, some of which brought them right up to the limits of airspace claimed by Libya, but there was no response from Tripoli.

Relations between Italy and Libya deteriorated, particularly during the crisis that erupted on 21 September 1973, when Italian Navy corvette *Visintini* (F546) – a ship of Pietro de Christofaro-class – was sailing in the Sicilian Strait. Around 1430 local time, the ship detected a pair of LAAF Mirage 5 fighter-bombers at a range of 33 nautical miles (61.1km). The two Libyan aircraft approached the Italian ship and opened fire with 30mm DEFA cannons, scoring several hits and injuring one sailor. After reporting this attack, the *Visintini's* skipper was ordered to maintain position and wait for reinforcements. However, before these could arrive on the scene, the Italian corvette was re-attacked by another pair of Mirages, which this time killed one and injured another sailor. Finally, the Italians returned fire with the OTO-Melara 76mm calibre cannon installed on the bow of their ship, and the Mirages withdrew. The damaged corvette was escorted to Sicily by two Italian destroyers, while Tripoli subsequently expressed 'sad regret' for this 'error'.[19]

In reaction to this attack, the Italian Air Force (Aeronautica Militare [Italiana], AMI) launched Operation Trinacria, deploying several brand-new Aeritalia-Lockheed F-104S Starfighters from the X Gruppo/9th Stormo (10th Squadron/9th Wing) to Trapani/Birgi Air Base (AB). They also rebuilt and extended the old runway on the island of Pantelleria, about 185km (115 miles) north

Before the arrival of Starfighters at Trapani/Birgi AB in 1972, the Italian Air Force was still using old North American F-86K Sabres for air defence purposes over Sicily. (Albert Grandolini Collection)

of Libya, making it suitable for deployment of Fiat G.91 and G.91Y light strikers, crews of which were specially trained for anti-ship operations. Over the following weeks and months, Starfighters in Sicily were regularly replaced by deployments from other AMI units based in central and northern Italy. Each detachment usually consisted of four or five aircraft armed with AIM-7E Sparrow and AIM-9B Sidewinder air-to-air missiles. Operation Trinacria only ended in 1993.

Despite such negative experiences, subsequent governments in Rome expressed significant interest in cooperation with Libya. Indeed, during the mid-1970s, Italy signed several huge arms contracts with Libya, including one for delivery of 20 Boeing-Meridionali CH-47 heavy helicopters and one for 240 SIAI-Marchetti SF.260WL training aircraft. When Tripoli insisted on not only buying, but also locally assembling SF.260s, the Italians proved more than happy to please: an agreement was reached for the SIAI to establish an appropriate facility at Sebha AB in Libya, staffed by Italian civilian technicians who trained and supervised Libyan personnel. While the Italians manufactured the first 60 SF.260WLs, the remaining 180 aircraft were delivered in the form of knock-down kits and assembled in Libya.[20]

Within the frame of the huge order for SF.260s, SIAI-Marchetti reached an agreement with Libya about maintenance and training of Libyan personnel. This necessitated the deployment of a team of Italian pilots and ground personnel to Libya. For this purpose – and supervised by the Head of the Italian Military Intelligence (Servizio Informazioni Militari, SIM), General Giuseppe Santovito (who also oversaw most Italian arms deals with Libya) – SIAI-Marchetti set up a subsidiary named Aero Leasing Italiana (ALI) at Roma Ciampino International Airport in September 1977. Run by Paolo Moci, a retired general of the Italian Air Force, ALI maintained only a small office, a single hangar, two Dassault Falcon 20s and a Learjet at Ciampino: its primary task was to recruit Italian personnel for SIAI-Marchetti's business in Libya. Screening interviews were carried out by another retired AMI general, Mario Tortora.

The majority of the first group of 60 pilots recruited by ALI had just been discharged from the AMI, and were contracted for 30 months, with an option for extension as necessary. As well as a handsome pay of between US$4,000 –5,000 a month, benefits

Up to 50 out of 240 SF.260WLs purchased by Libya remained in service with the LAAF in the twenty-first century. As well as for training purposes, the type saw intensive service as light strikers during LAAF deployments in Chad. (Tom Cooper Collection)

In late 1979, and for most of 1980, sizeable detachments of LAAF helicopters were based at Luqa IAP on Malta. This example, serialled LC-157, is seen on 14 March 1980. (Hugues Deguillebon Collection)

Following their basic training on SF.260s with the help for Italian instructors, future LAAF fighter pilots continued training on Yugoslav-made SOKO G-2 Galebs, 50 of which were acquired in the early 1970s. This example was photographed at Misurata Air Force Academy Base. (Vaclav Havner via Albert Grandolini)

Another of the Libyan Super Frelons temporarily deployed to Malta was this example, an SA.321GM with serial number LC-194, seen in December 1980. Some Libyan helicopters – including three Aérospatiale SE.316B Alouette IIIs and one of the Super Frelons – were impounded at Malta after the Libyans were expelled from the island. The Alouettes were put into Maltese service after a corresponding agreement with Tripoli in the early 1990s. (Hugues Deguillebon Collection)

included one month of leave and three free trips to Italy per annum. ALI not only provided for all of their living expenses in Libya, but also provided housing – including flats for those who decided to take their families with them.

On arrival in Libya, the Italians were grouped at Sebha AB, where they were told they had replaced a similar-sized group of Yugoslav instructors. Constructed in the mid-1970s, Sebha already included installations, offices and housing for a Basic Flying School. The Italians found it relatively easy to develop a training syllabus for 100 pilots a year, all trained on SF.260s, which included not only basic flying but also air-to-ground attack exercises with machine guns, rockets and light bombs at the nearby bombing range.

The Malta Affair

Midway through the working up of ALI's mission to Libya, another crisis erupted between Rome and Tripoli in the wake of Maltese independence from Great Britain in March 1979.

The first government of an independent Malta refused repeated requests from London to grant basing permissions for British military, and instead showed interest in accepting economic aid from Libya – including oil provided at favourable terms. A small Libyan military contingent was deployed on the island, including a detachment of Aérospatiale SA.321 Super Frelon helicopters equipped for search and rescue (SAR) purposes, and LAAF personnel manned the local air traffic control and associated radars. This Libyan move was perceived as a threat to the 'southern flank' of the North Atlantic Treaty Organisation (NATO), which

began developing concerns that, via the Libyan connection, Malta might grant basing rights for warships of the Soviet Navy. In order to prevent something of this kind, Italy offered generous economic aid to Malta, in exchange for the island's neutrality and a guarantee that the Maltese would grant basing rights to neither the Americans or the Soviets. The Maltese government agreed, but its decision was greeted with suspicion by Tripoli – even more so once the islanders announced their intention to explore the possible offshore oil deposits in the Medina Shoals, halfway between Malta and Libya.

The Libyans, who were already involved in similar operations in the same area, issued a fierce protest over such intentions, and the Maltese requested the Italian ENI Oil Company to run preliminary exploration work instead. Not only did this decision result in a break-down of diplomatic relations between Rome and Tripoli, but Ghaddafi then ordered his navy into action. On 10 July 1980, two Italian fishing boats were stopped and confiscated by Libyan warships – allegedly for entering Libyan territorial waters. The 19 sailors from the two vessels were arrested, and only released two years later.

On 2 August 1980, Italy and Malta signed a friendship treaty, and two days later an alleged coup attempt took place in Tripoli. Ghaddafi accused Italy of involvement in the plot and Libyan authorities arrested three Italian businessmen; they were only released six years later and it eventually turned out that one of

An Atlantic maritime partrol aircraft (MPA) of the 41st Stormo against the backdrop of Mount Etna, on Sicily, sometime in the early 1980s. The type was primarily responsible for tracking the activity of Libyan and Soviet submarines on approaches to the Gulf of Taranto. (Albert Grandolini Collection)

A pair of AMI F-104 Starfighters – armed with AIM-7 Sparrow and AIM-9 Sidewinder missiles – scrambling from Trapani/Birgi AB in 1983. (Albert Grandolini Collection)

them was indeed an Italian intelligence officer.

Meanwhile, a Libyan warship and a Foxtrot-class submarine began shadowing the oil exploration ship *Saipem 2*, chartered by ENI for operations in the Medina Shoals area, on 24 August 1980. After the Libyans threatened to open fire, *Saipem 2* left the area – but later returned under escort from two Italian warships. The situation remained tense for several days, eventually prompting the AMI to launch F-104G Starfighter interceptors from Trapani/ Birgi AB in western Sicily for patrols over the area. Simultaneously, Maltese armed forces were put on full alert.

While tensions subsequently dissipated, the AMI extended its air defence operations to Maltese airspace under Operations Erice and Vento Caldo (Hot Wind). These included setting up an Air Defence Operation Cell (Nucleo Operativo di Difesa Aerea, NODA) to supervise all relevant operations over the island and surrounding areas with the help of radars connected via the NATO Air Defence Ground Environment (NADGE) system, starting on 1 September 1983. During the same year, the Italian Army deployed an air defence battalion equipped with MIM-23B I-HAWK SAMs near Trapani/Birgi AB. The F-104-detachment based at Trapani/Birgi AB was eventually increased to 16 interceptors and expanded into a new fighter wing – the 37th Stormo – effective from 1 October 1984, by when the base housed

a combat, search and rescue (CSAR) element – the 82nd Centro CSAR – consisting of six Agusta-Sikorsky HH-3F helicopters from the 15th Stormo.

The establishment of the 37th Stormo did not replace the rotational deployment system of other F-104-equipped units. On the contrary, detachments from other wings maintained a near-permanent presence at Trapani/Birgi, greatly easing the burden of the unit permanently stationed at that base. Along with Italian interceptors, Trapani/Birgi saw regular deployments of Boeing E-3A Sentry airborne warning and control system (AWACS) aircraft of the US Air Force (USAF) and Piaggio PD.808GE electronic warfare of the AMI. Bréguet Br.1150 Atlantic maritime patrol aircraft (MPAs) of the 30th and 41st Stormo began flying regular patrols south of Sicily in order to counter any potential threats by Libyan – and Soviet – submarines, especially on approaches to the strategically important Gulf of Taranto.[21]

Considering these and other incidents that took place in this part of the Mediterranean cited in Part 1 of this mini-series, it was unsurprising that the White House and Pentagon eventually decided to demonstrate US military might through a freedom of navigation (FON) exercise in the Gulf of Syrte in August 1981.

Italian Instructors in Libya

Ignoring such 'thorny issues', the governments in Rome and Tripoli remained insistent on safeguarding the existing contracts between the LAAF and SIAI-Marchetti. During the stand-off over Malta, ALI's instructors continued their work. The Italian company even intensified its operations in Libya, and in 1980 redeployed parts of its team to Ghat AB, to open another flying school. By this time, no less than 140 Italian instructor pilots had already served in Libya, graduating 310 Libyan pilots after a total of about 37,000 flying hours.

In 1981, Rome and Tripoli signed a contract for delivery of 20 Aeritalia G.222L light transports. In support of this deal, the ALI further increased its team in Libya and set up a provisional detachment of instructors and SF.260s at the LAAF Academy in Misurata, where they helped train a new intake of Libyan cadets destined to fly new, Italian-made transports. The Libyan G.222 order prompted the Italians to set up a dedicated instructor team, once again primarily consisting of former AMI pilots. Because of a US embargo from 1981, Aeritalia was forced to replace the original General Electric T-64-P4D engines of the G.222 with Rolls Royce Tyne Mk.801s. While delivering nearly two times as much power as the US-made engines, Tynes consumed significantly more fuel, reducing the range of the aircraft by nearly a third. However, Aeritalia not only failed to properly test-fly the new version, but also provided flight and technical manuals for older variants without any advice about possible problems resulting from installation of Rolls Royce engines.

This became particularly obvious when the LAAF's brand-new G.222Ls were rushed into service in support of Libyan involvement in Chad: before long, several G.222Ls were forced to make emergency landings in the desert, all caused by fuel starvation. While it took Italian instructors and their Libyan cadets – nearly all of whom were fresh out of conversion courses on SF.260s and Antonov An-26s – some time to develop new procedures to operate the type effectively, an early solution for emergency landings in the desert was found in the form of making 'touch and go' landings to test the firmness of soil!

Meanwhile, Italian SF.260 instructors had quite different experiences during their tours in Libya. One of the negative aspects of ALI's mission in that country was the 'unwritten' clause that Italians could be mobilised 'for border patrol duty' – which actually meant that they could be requested to engage in combat operations if the Libyans deemed this necessary. In autumn 1980, Libya ordered a particularly experienced ex-AMI fighter pilot to deploy to Chad for combat operations. When not only the pilot in question, but also ALI's Chief Pilot, Sarti, refused to obey this order, the Libyans threatened to expel the entire team. Eventually, even at the height of the Malta affair, Rome and Tripoli found a compromise: Italian pilots ferried SF.260s to the Aouzou airfield, where they were picked up by Libyans for deployment to Chad.

Additional problems emerged when the LAAF began returning SF.260s for regular maintenance to Sebha. It turned out that Libyan pilots and ground personnel seldom filed flying hours into technical log books of their aircraft, and rarely – if at all – reported any defects. One such case resulted in the death of Italian pilot Maresciallo Giuseppe Frescura, who lost the tailplane during a post-maintenance test-flight and crashed. The ALI investigation into the reasons for this fatal incident concluded that the aircraft suffered structural damage caused by repeated hard landings on primitive strips in Chad, but that nobody reported this in technical documentation.

One of the Italian instructor pilots in Libya was Andrea Tamburro, a former officer of the Italian Army Aviation with experience on SIAI-Marchetti SM.1019s. He signed a contract with ALI immediately after leaving the military and underwent a conversion course on SF.260s at Vergiate, being told that if he completed this successfully, he would be hired for a job that would pay all the costs of training. After successfully completing his

Because they were acquired at the time Libya began to suffer from ever-sharper US embargoes, and flown by inexperienced novices, the 20 RR Tyne-powered G.222Ls of the LAAF saw a relatively brief but intensive service. This example with serial number 223 nicely illustrates details of the bigger new engine of the variant. (Albert Grandolini Collection)

Dozens of 240 SF.260s acquired from Italy in the late 1970s were used for ground training at Sebha AB, under tutelage of Italian instructors. (Tom Cooper Collection)

training, Tamburro signed a contract for six months and was put on a Libyan Arab Airlines Boeing 727 that brought him to Tripoli, from where he continued the trip to Sebha AB. Although arriving at his new job in the middle of the summer holidays, when when most Libyan cadets and their Italian instructors were on leave, he soon found himself in charge of several young cadets flying two training missions a day. Occasionally, he would be redeployed to Ghat AB to reinforce the team of instructors there.

Through 1981, the majority of Italian instructors – about 50 of them – remained at Sebha, while about 30 were usually at Ghat. They were working eight hours a day, six days a week and taught LAAF cadets roughly following the training syllabus of the AMI. For various reasons – primarily related to language issues – there were some differences. For example, while Italian military pilots were expected to make their first solo flight on their 18th mission, Libyans usually did so during their 25th or 30th mission. A typical working day began at 0600, and most of the flying took place during the morning because of the growing heat later during the day. Whenever temperatures reached 40° Celsius, all flights were cancelled. Most instructors made two or three flights a day. Afternoons were reserved for ground instructions, and all lectures were provided in English. The Italians concluded that most Libyan pilots were 'average', and could never stop wondering about the poor educational background of many of them, or the fact that many Libyan students were not keen to join the military, and even less so to become military pilots. As the training progressed, there were numerous accidents, mostly during the cross-country navigational flight Sebha – Ghat –Sebha, during which quite a

A rare 'air-to-air' photograph showing a Mirage 5DD two-seat conversion trainer, serial number 201, leading a pair of Mirage 5Ds (410 in foreground and 401 or 421 in centre) during a training flight in the 1980s. (Pit Weinert Collection)

The Mirage 5D still represented the most important fighter-bomber type in LAAF service during the early 1980s. Serial number 421 is shown at Misurata Air Force Academy Air Base.
(Vaclav Havner via Albert Grandolini)

One of 32 Mirage 5DE interceptors acquired by Libya, after overhauls in France, in July 1981. Each of the three LAAF units equipped with this type operated a mix of 5DE interceptors and other variants.
(Stefane Mellec)

few LAAF cadets got lost and were forced to make emergency landings in the desert. Eventually, no less than 204 additional pilots graduated from Italian-run flight schools in 1981.

During the following year, the number of Italian instructors decreased to about 38, but they were supplemented by 15 Libyan instructors trained at Varese – near SIAI-Marchetti's main production facility for SF.260s.

Unfinished Force: LAAF in 1985

Unlike in the 1970s, when Libya was purchasing immense numbers of new combat aircraft, massive investment in training of new pilots with the help of Czechoslovak and Italian instructors did not go hand in hand with additional acquisitions of fighter jets. Instead, the pace of new Libyan orders decreased significantly during the early 1980s, primarily because of worsening relations with Western powers, but also because – as described above – the LAAF concentrated on training pilots and ground crews for what was on hand.

Although still in possession of about 90 such aircraft, the LAAF kept only about 60 Mirage 5 fighters in operational condition at any given time. These comprised the primary equipment of four squadrons. Three operational units were colloquially known as Shaheen, Qods and Yarmouk. Two of these were based at Mitiga (together with most of the technical support equipment) and one at el-Woutia. Each unit operated a mix of Mirage 5D fighter-bombers, Mirage 5DE interceptors and Mirage 5DR reconnaissance fighters. French reports cited that Mirage 5DRs were rarely used in their intended role: instead, they were usually flown as 'advanced trainers', enabling pilots fresh from conversion courses to gain experience on single-seat variants, or for navigational training. Mirage 5DD two-seat conversion trainers were all assigned to the dedicated Operational Conversion Unit

(OCU). Despite increasing tensions between France and Libya – especially because of the situation in Chad, some 85 percent of Libyan Mirage 5s were sent to France for overhauls between 1977 and 1985.[22]

El-Woutia was also the home of two units equipped with Mirage F.1AD fighter-bombers, Mirage F.1ED interceptors and Mirage F.1BD two-seat conversion trainers. About eight Mirage F.1ADs and two F.1BDs were operational with No. 1011 Squadron on average, while 11 Mirage F.1EDs and one or two F.1BDs were usually operational with No. 1012 Squadron (also known as 'Fatah Squadron'). All the maintenance facilities and a vast stock of spares were concentrated at el-Woutia, but LAAF Mirage F.1-units frequently maintained temporary detachments at Gamal Abdel Nasser AB south of Tobruq. Having its own bombing range nearby, el-Woutia was intensively used for most ground-attack related exercises by all Mirage-equipped squadrons. Reports that there were only six fully qualified Libyan pilots available to fly all the Mirage F.1s of the two squadrons for most of the 1980s, and that these had to be backed up by a small number of French and other foreign pilots, cannot be confirmed. On the contrary, Libyan reports stress that No. 1011 and No. 1012 Squadrons were staffed by some of the best LAAF pilots and officers, while even Soviet sources stress that Libyans were paying much more attention to maintenance of their French-made aircraft than they did to Soviet-delivered aircraft.[23]

Gamal Abdel Nasser AB remained the home of No. 1021 Squadron, which was the sole unit operating survivors of the 64 MiG-21bis and MiG-21UMs acquired by Libya in the mid-1970s. Overall, very little is known about the activities of this unit in the 1980s, by when it seems that the majority of LAAF MiG-21s were used as advanced trainers – whether for Libyan or the many foreign pilots trained in Libya. Reports that up to 30 Libyan MiG-

A pair of LAAF MiG-21bis (serial number 500 on the left and 454 on the right), together with their pilots and ground crews at Kufra AB, in southern Libya, in the late 1980s. (Pit Weinert Collection)

A row of Mirage F.1AD fighter-bombers, 16 of which were purchased by Libya, shown shortly before their delivery in 1979. (Marcel Fluet-Lecerf)

The first of 16 Mirage F.1ED interceptors acquired by Libya – serial number 501 – during a pre-delivery test-flight. Like most of the LAAF's Mirage F.1-fleet, this aircraft saw relatively short but intensive service during the 1980s. As of 2015, it was last seen stripped down and stored inside an overhaul facility at Tripoli IAP. (Marcel Fluet-Lecerf)

This Mirage F.1DD two-seat conversion trainer (serial number 205) was one of only six such aircraft acquired by Libya. At least two of these were written off during the 1980s, while one was eventually destroyed by NATO air strikes in 2011. (Marcel Fluet-Lecerf)

21bis aircraft were provided to Syria following its heavy losses in air combat over Lebanon in June 1982 remain unconfirmed.

The number of remaining MiG-23MS interceptors had decreased significantly because of the many accidents with them in the 1970s. After Syria lost four MiG-21bis' in a clash with McDonnell Douglas F-15A Eagle interceptors of the Israeli Defence Force/Air Force (IDF/AF) over Lebanon in 1979, Gaddafi had turned over a batch of four MiG-23MS aircraft to the SyAAF.

At least 12 additional MiG-23MS were provided to Syria in late 1982, when they were replaced by about 20 improved MiG-23MF interceptors, and a few additional MiG-23UBs used to replace losses through attrition. By 1986, the LAAF received a similar-sized batch of more advanced MiG-23ML interceptors.

Prompted by Soviet boasts, the Libyans expected the new MiG-23MFs and MiG-23MLs to prove a major improvement in comparison to the poorly-armed MiG-23MSs. Although carrying less fuel, both variants were equipped with vastly improved radars and air-to-air missiles (AAMs) theoretically capable of engaging targets beyond visual range (BVR). Former LAAF MiG-23 pilot Ali Thani described the two new variants introduced into service with No 1023 Squadron (MiG-23ML, based at Mitiga) and No. 1050 Squadron (which flew MiG-23MFs based at the newly-constructed al-Bumbah AB, west of Tobruq) and their new armament as follows:

Soviets were full of praise for their new R-23R missile [ASCC-code AA-7 Apex; authors' note], especially its infra-red homing variant, which was said to possess advanced capabilities of countering infra-red decoys. Actually, this weapon proved a big failure and we replaced it as soon as the R-24 arrived, together with MiG-23MLs, in 1985. The R-24 missile was a major improvement in comparison to [the] R-23. It was much more reliable and had a higher probability of [a] hit. Still, the best weapon of both [the] MiG-23MF and MiG-23ML was the R-60MK [ASCC-code AA-8 Aphid; authors' note], which had a very wide engagement envelope and was simple to deploy, even if its range was quite limited.

Our MiG-23MFs were equipped with S-23E radar and TP-26 infra-red search and track system (IRST). [The] Soviets told us the radar could detect targets out to 60km away but we could seldom detect American fighters at further than 40-45km. Detection range very much depended on good work of electronics-specialists in our squadron: the S-23E required lots of expert tuning. Some specialists were better, others not, and thus detection ranges often varied from aircraft to aircraft, sometimes by up to 10km. In engagements with Americans, the S-23E proved capable of detecting targets at longer ranges than Cyrano radars of our Mirages, but [was] also severely vulnerable to electronic countermeasures. Foremost, it proved prone to malfunctions. We tried to work with the TP-26 and tested it extensively, but never detected anything beyond the range of 15km – slightly more in clear weather and at high altitude.

A group of young LAAF pilots in front of MiG-21UM serial number 108 in the early 1980s. The type was used for the training of Libyan and various foreign pilots trained in Libya. (Pit Weinert Collection)

Libyan pilot with a MiG-23MS at Benina AB in the early 1980s. (via Pit Weinert)

Clandestinely taken photograph of one of the first MiG-23MLs delivered to Libya, taken at Mitiga AB, in Tripoli, in early 1986. (Albert Grandolini Collection)

The MiG-23ML was a very fine aircraft, with lighter fuselage, different tail section, new landing gear and an uprated engine that made it much safer to fly and more manoeuvrable. It came with a fourth wing-setting of 33 degrees, in addition to [the] usual positions of 16, 45 and 72 degrees. We found this setting of 33 degrees best suited for combat manoeuvring. Its N008 Saphir-ML radar was 170kg lighter than the N003 on [the] MiG-23MF. It had dogfight modes, a full look-down/shoot down mode and an effective range

Two young Libyan pilots and one of the brand-new MiG-25PDS interceptors (serial number 6801) in February 1986. (Pit Weinert Collection)

of 50km. It could track up to six targets simultaneously, and was an overall improvement over S-23E on [the] MiG-23MF. However, when [a] pilot locked-on one target the others would disappear from the HUD, making it easy to lose situational awareness. Even more troublesome was its reliability. N008 tended to malfunction shortly after achieving a lock-on. Both problems were related to [a] weak computer supporting the radar.

Deliveries of MiG-25s to Libya concluded with the arrival of a large batch of MiG-25PDSs in the early 1980s, bringing the fleet of interceptors to about 60 airframes – in addition to six each of MiG-25R reconnaissance fighters and MiG-25PU two-seat conversion trainers. Although actually based on overhauled MiG-25P aircraft, the PDS variant was a significant improvement over the older MiG-25P version delivered to the LAAF from 1979 because of its upgraded Smerch 2A (range 100km), addition of the TP-26Sh-1 IRST system, more reliable engines and capability to carry up to four R-60MK AAMs in addition to two R-40s (ASCC-code AA-6 Acrid). The range and speed of the MiG-25, coupled with the long range and massive punch of its R-40s, made this type an aircraft from which many – Libyans and their Soviet advisors – expected a lot. The LAAF MiG-25s not only confronted USN pilots over the Gulf of Syrte in 1981, but flew intensive operations over Chad during the early 1980s.

Out of five Libyan squadrons originally planned to operate MiG-25s, only four are known to have become operational. The majority of the older MiG-25Ps and MiG-25PU two-seat conversion trainers were meanwhile in service with No. 1005 and 1025 Squadrons at al-Jufra/Hun AB. Most of the MiG-25PDS were operated by the Mitiga-based No. 1035 Squadron, while No. 1015 Squadron worked up at el-Woutia AB before being redeployed to Ghurdabiyah/Syrte in 1983 or 1985.

Apart from Mirages and MiGs, the LAAF still operated about 30 Su-22 and Su-22Ms, organised into two squadrons: No. 1022 at Ghurdabiyah/Syrte and No. 1032 Squadron at el-Woutia. Despite reports about deliveries of up to 100 Sukhois through the early 1980s, the third unit usually associated with this type – No. 1036 Squadron – appears to have never reached operational status.

The major striking force of the LAAF therefore remained

A Czechoslovak instructor with three Libyan pilots from No. 1039 Squadron, LAAF, and one of their L-39ZOs (serial number 1940) at Wadi Doum AB, in northern Chad, in the mid-1980s. (Vaclav Havner)

One of about a dozen Antonov An-26 transports acquired by Libya from 1980. After a period of being used as advanced trainers for future transport pilots at Misurata AB, they saw extensive service all over Africa. (Albert Grandolini Collection)

A rare photograph of one of the few early Mi-24As delivered to Libya in the late 1970s. Nothing is known about the number of such helicopters acquired by the LAAF, nor their fate. They would have been camouflaged in standard Soviet 'sand and spinach' colours. (Pit Weinert Collection)

Libya acquired an unknown quantity of Mi-8s in the late 1970s, which served as true workhorses of the LAAF for years. This example is from the late 2000s at Mitiga AB. (Milipix/Martin Hornliman Collection)

a squadron of 12 Tupolev Tu-22 bombers based at al-Jufra/Hun AB. Deployed in action during wars between Uganda and Tanzania in 1979, in Chad and Sudan in 19811983, this unit was to see intensive action during the coming years.

However, all of these aircraft and their crews remained imposing only on paper. In reality, the LAAF – now under the command of Colonel Salleh Abdullah Salleh – remained unable to run exercises at operational level in 1985 and 1986. Indeed, not one of its squadrons flew any major exercises in either of these years: all the operational training was limited to tactical training of individual pilots in a simplified environment. This meant that the LAAF's pilots and ground controllers remained unable to fight in larger formations than a pair, and that – with a mere handful of exceptions – they were not trained to operate by night. Perhaps more importantly, Libyan pilots never trained for operations in cooperation with ground-based air defences. Indeed, it seems that even as of spring 1986, the LAAF still had no centralised command structure, even on single air bases, and next to no joint training, even between neighbouring fighter squadrons.

Under such circumstances, the conclusion is that the relatively large counterinsurgency (COIN) element of the LAAF – comprising units equipped with SF.260s, L-39s and Mi-25s – was probably the most effective part of the entire air force. Completely staffed by Libyans – though working under some Czechoslovak supervision – this was to provide valuable services during the fighting in Chad in the late 1980s.

At least as important for that conflict was the provision of the LAAF's extensive transport facilities, mainly the squadrons equipped with Il-76s.

Transport and Helicopter Fleets

Early Libyan experiences from the war in Chad had proven the value of transport aircraft and helicopters for support of ground operations in the Sahara desert, so the LAAF spent much of the early 1980s acquiring related aircraft and equipment and training in the use of such equipment.

Out of eight Lockheed C-130H Hercules transports originally introduced into service by No. 1230 Squadron, seven were still intact (serial number 116 was lost in Uganda in 1979). Although a US arms embargo prevented the LAAF from receiving eight other C-130Hs, the Libyans managed to acquire at least four aircraft of civilian variant designated Lockheed L-100-20. Nevertheless, it seems that the plan to equip three of their C-130s for ELINT/SIGINT purposes and as aircraft for stand-off electronic countermeasures (ECM) with help from France appears to have never been realised.

During the late 1970s, the LAAF began purchasing Ilyushin Il-76 jet transports from the USSR. The exact number of these acquired remains unclear, because many of the 25 or so aircraft of this type identified at this time were frequently operated on behalf of civilian and para-military companies. Apart from the above-mentioned 20 G.222s and 19 L-410 Turbolet light transports, the LAAF acquired up to 20 Antonov An-26 transports of Soviet origin, starting in 1980, together with a facility equipped for their overhaul.

As reported in Part 1 of this mini-series, the original helicopter fleet of the LAAF primarily consisted of French-made helicopters, such as 18 Aérospatiale SE.316B Alouette IIIs and 13 Aérospatiale SA.321M/GM Super Frelons. From the mid-1970s, the Libyan Arab Army purchased a number of Agusta-Bell 205A-1s and Agusta-Bell 206A light helicopters from Italy, followed by 20 Boeing-Meridionali CH-47C Chinooks.

Nearly all Libyan helicopter crews were trained by a group of Polish advisors at Misurata AB, on Mil Mi-2 light helicopters of Soviet origin. Libyans purchased enough Mil Mi-8 transport helicopters, Mi-24A and Mi-25 helicopter gunships to equip a total of four squadrons.

With very few exceptions, nearly all of these transport aircraft and helicopters were to see extensive service in Chad during the second half of the 1980s. Indeed, the transport branch of the LAAF was the best-developed element of this air force in 1985–1986; squadrons equipped with Il-76s, C-130s and CH-47s were to provide excellent service to Libyan ground forces there.

CHAPTER 2
TERROR IN THE SKIES

While no Libya-related terrorist attacks were observed by US intelligence agencies in the aftermath of the clash between US Navy Tomcats and LAAF Sukhois in August 1981, or through 1982 and 1983, tensions between Tripoli and Washington began to increase because Gaddafi initiated a number of operations that directly challenged major Western powers – especially the USA. He began providing economic aid and arms to the government of the leftist Sandinista National Liberation Front (Frente Sandinista de Liberación Nacional, FSLN) in Nicaragua, which was fighting a Washington-supported centrist insurgency, in 1983. In April 1983, three Libyan Il-76TD and a C-130 landed at Manaus airport in Brazil after one of them developed technical problems. When Brazilian authorities inspected all four aircraft, they found crates with 17 disassembled Aero L-39s bound for Nicaragua, instead of the 'medical supplies' quoted in transport documentation.[24] Nevertheless, other Libyan shipments of arms – including at least seven SF.260s and a significant consignment of SA-7 MANPADS – did reach Nicaragua in 1984 and 1985.

In March 1984, four bombs exploded near the homes of Libyan exiles or in businesses frequented by them in London and Manchester. In April of the same year, a person inside the Libyan 'People's Bureau' (Libyan Embassy) in London opened machine-gun fire at a group of about 70 Libyan anti-Gaddafi protesters, killing a British policewoman. London promptly expelled all Libyan diplomats and severed diplomatic relations with Tripoli. During the summer of 1984, persuasive circumstantial evidence linked the Libyan roll-on/roll-off ship SS Ghat to the mining of shipping lanes in the Gulf of Suez, which caused indiscriminate damage to at least 18 merchant vessels. In September 1984, the Libyan secret service attempted to assassinate President Hissène Habrè of Chad and blow up the US Embassy in Cairo. They subsequently began assaulting Libyan exiles in Egypt.[25]

Despite a Franco-Libyan agreement about disengagement from Chad, from November 1984, and the withdrawal of their troops from that country, French military reconnaissance and several US intelligence agencies continued carefully monitoring Libyan behaviour. Before long it was obvious that although French troops had departed the country, Gaddafi deceived Paris: his troops only withdrew into northern Chad, where they bivouacked in concealed positions. Around the same time, Libyan relations with the government of the Islamic Republic of Iran became so close that Tripoli began providing ballistic missiles and other heavy armament to Tehran (for details on missiles in question, see separate box below), in cooperation with Syria.

Through the same time, covert US operations to destabilise Gaddafi's government achieved very little. A group of Libyan dissidents trained in Sudan did launch a coup attempt after infiltrating Libya from Tunisia, on 8 May 1984. However, three of them were captured shortly after and revealed all the details of the operation to Libyan authorities, and this effort ended in the course of a five-hour fire-fight in Tripoli before any of the plotters could assault Gaddafi's residence inside the Bab al-Aziziya Barracks. Subsequently, Libyan security services not only purged the entire military, arrested thousands and hanged hundreds of suspects, but Gaddafi allowed the Soviets greater access to Libyan military facilities: while Soviet maritime patrol aircraft began operating out of Mitiga to monitor the movement of US and allied warships in the Mediterranean, Soviet warships were granted permission to perform repairs in Tobruq. After Jafar an-Numayri was ousted in a coup in April 1985, Gaddafi renewed diplomatic ties to Sudan and exploited the opportunity to not only prevent the establishment of a parliamentary democracy there, but also began providing arms, funding and training to a small insurgent group dedicated to the establishment of a Libyan-style government.[26]

Spring of Hijackings

Gaddafi did not limit his actions to subversion of neighbouring states and assassinations of Libyan exiles. A CIA Study from March 1985 concluded that Libya became involved in providing support to radical political movements, insurgent groups and terrorist organisations active or based in Antigua, Austria, Bangladesh, Benin, Chad, Costa Rica, Dominica, El Salvador, Ghana, Great

Britain, Guatemala, Honduras, the Dominican Republic, Chile, Colombia, Iraq, Kenya, Lebanon, Namibia, Nicaragua, Niger, Nigeria, Oman, Pakistan, the Philippines, Somalia, Spain, St Lucia, Tunisia, Uganda and Zaire.[27] As if to confirm the findings of that study, a series of hijackings of international airliners over the Mediterranean Sea and surrounding countries was to follow during the following months. While most of them were related to the ongoing civil war in Lebanon and the Arab-Israeli confrontation, and were usually easier to link with Syria or even Iran than with Libya, few were directly linked to Gaddafi. With nobody else providing as much money, weapons, training and refuge to terrorist groups around the world, broadcasting inflammatory public appeals for attacks on USA and threats of blood and death, while also being the most isolated and the weakest in terms of military capabilities, the Libyan leader clearly exposed himself to a counter-attack.

As usual, this was only one part of the background for what was going on in and over the Mediterranean in 1985 and 1986. Another major part was the Israeli decision to withdraw from southern Lebanon, announced in January 1985. After conquering this part of its northern neighbour relatively quickly in June 1982, and enforcing the deportation of the PLO from Beirut two months later, the Israelis subsequently found themselves involved in a long, bloody and costly war with new enemies in Lebanon, mainly the Iranian-supported Hezbollah. Immense spending for continuous war, the vast expansion of Israeli Defence Forces, but also the inability to pacify the area under IDFs control, eventually caused rampant inflation and brought the Israeli economy to the brink of collapse. The Israeli pull-out was not complete: a significant IDF force was left inside southern Lebanon to maintain a buffer zone along the border with Israel.

Israeli withdrawal created a power-vacuum in central and eastern Lebanon, rapidly filled by Hezbollah and another militia of Lebanese Shi'a, the Amal Movement. Their presence was to be felt very soon. On 7 February 1985, four Lebanese Shi'a armed with automatic weapons stormed the Boeing 707-123B of Cyprus Airways at the apron of Beirut IAP, taking a crew of nine and three Lebanese employees of KLM Royal Dutch Airlines as hostages. The hijackers demanded the release of two Lebanese men jailed in Cyprus for the hijacking of a Romanian airliner in 1983. The hostages and the aircraft were released after several hours, when the Cypriot government agreed to consider the hijackers' demands.

On 27 March 1985, a Lufthansa Boeing 727-230 with 143 passengers and eight 8 crew was hijacked by a lone male while flying from Munich in Germany to Athens in Greece, and diverted to Libya. When the pilot advised the hijacker that the aircraft did not have sufficient fuel to reach Libya, the hijacker forced him to land at Istanbul in Turkey instead. Two hours after landing, Turkish security personnel boarded the aircraft and overpowered the hijacker.

Less than a week later, on 1 April, a Boeing 707-300 of Middle East Airlines (MEA) with 66 passengers and 10 crew aboard was hijacked en-route from Beirut to Jeddah. The Lebanese hijacker demanded payment of several million dollars for Hezbollah until security authorities persuaded him to give up, after landing at Jeddah.

Two months later, on 11 June, a Boeing 727-2D3 of Alia Royal Jordanian Airlines was hijacked by five Lebanese Shi'a between Beirut and Amman. The hijackers demanded to be flown to Tunis, but Tunisian authorities refused landing permission and the flight diverted to Palermo IAP on Sicily. After refuelling there, the aircraft was flown back to Beirut. It took off early in the morning of the next day, but then returned: all occupants – including a crew of nine, eight sky-marshals and 65 passengers were released and the Boeing then blown up using explosives. Also on 11 June, a MEA Boeing 707-300 was hijacked by a lone Palestinian shortly before landing at Larnaca IAP. All 166 passengers and five of the 10 crew members were set free after landing. The hijacker stated that his action was in retaliation for the hijacking of the Alia airliner and demanded the release of the eight sky-marshals. When informed that these were not in custody, the hijacker gave himself up: he was allowed to board a nearby Royal Jordanian Airlines aircraft and was flown to Amman, where Jordanian authorities arrested him.

The next hijacking followed two days later. On 14 June, TWA Boeing 727-200 (registration N64339) on Flight 847 from Cairo via Athens, Rome and Boston to Los Angeles was hijacked by two members of Hezbollah after take-off from Athens. The hijackers demanded the release of 'Kuwait 17' (a group involved in the 1983 bombing of the US embassy in Kuwait), the release of 766 mainly Lebanese Shi'a Muslims from Israeli detention and international condemnation of Israel and the United States.[28] They diverted the flight to Beirut IAP, where 19 passengers were allowed to leave in exchange for fuel. Later the same afternoon, the aircraft took off again and flew across the Mediterranean to Algiers, in Algeria, where 20 further passengers were released during a five-hour stop. During the night, the aircraft flew back to Beirut. While demanding additional fuel the next morning, the hijackers beat and then murdered US Navy diver Robert Stethem and dumped his body out of the plane. Seven other American passengers, alleged to have Jewish-sounding surnames, were taken off the jet and held hostage in Beirut, while the hijackers were reinforced by about a dozen gunmen who entered the aircraft. After refuelling, the aircraft flew for Algiers again, where 65 passengers and all five female cabin crew members were released. The hijackers then demanded to fly to Tehran, but instead returned to Beirut on 16 June and remained there for unknown reasons. During the afternoon of 17 June, the 40 remaining hostages had been taken from the aircraft and distributed through the Hezbollah-held portions of Beirut.

Despite public announcements about the intention to deploy US military power against terrorism, President Reagan was forced to accept that there was no other solution than to negotiate. While putting special forces of the US Army and Navy on alert for a possible intervention, he opened negotiations with Damascus and Tel Aviv. The hostages were eventually released a fortnight later – apparently in exchange for the release of over 700 Lebanese

Shi'a prisoners by Israel – brought to Syria and then flown out to Germany.[29]

Wooden Leg

Despite their withdrawal from central and eastern Lebanon, the Israelis continued monitoring the situation in Lebanon very carefully. Above all determined to undermine any attempts by the PLO to return to Beirut, they deployed their navy to monitor Palestinian maritime traffic between the Lebanese capital and Cyprus. On 10 September 1985, an Israeli patrol boat with Mossad agents on board intercepted a small ship that regularly shuttled between Beirut and Larnaca, and arrested a senior officer of the PLO's elite Force 17. The officer was taken to Israel, interrogated, then tried and given a heavy prison sentence. In retaliation for this operation, gunmen from Force 17 hijacked an Israeli yacht off the coast of Larnaca and killed three Israelis on board on 25 September, claiming these were Mossad agents monitoring Palestinian naval traffic in the area. The attack shocked Israel and prompted its government to order an immediate retaliation – in the form of an air strike on the new PLO HQ, set up at Hamman ash-Shatt, near Tunis. The resulting Operation Wooden Leg was prepared with the help of intelligence provided by Jonathan Pollard, an officer of the US Navy's Naval Intelligence Command (NIC), who was arrested by the Federal Bureau of Investigation in November 1985.[30]

The strike was carried out on 1 October 1985 by six F-15B/D Eagle fighter-bombers from No. 106 'Spearhead' Squadron IDF/AF, each carrying one GBU-15 electro-optically guided bomb, the pod necessary for the guidance of such weapons and four AIM-7 Sparrow missiles. This formation was supported by four F-15Cs from No. 133 'Twin Tail' Squadron, armed with AIM-7 Sparrow and AIM-9 Sidewinder missiles, but also six Mk.82 bombs on a multiple-ejector rack installed under the centreline hardpoint, two of which acted as spares. All 10 Eagles took off at 0800 local time to meet with two Boeing 707 tankers about an hour later. After refuelling, eight F-15s continued in the direction of Tunisia, followed by a third Boeing 707 that acted as an airborne command post, while two spares returned home.

Underway towards Tunisia, the Israelis overflew the Italian islands of Lampedusa and Pantelleria, which they used to update their INS navigational systems.[31] The formation then split into two flights of four, separated by four minutes, while approaching the target zone. By this time, two Eagles experienced various failures of their avionics and the other crews were forced to re-distribute targets between them. Eventually, the first three F-15B/Ds released their GBU-15s from about 20–25km and an altitude of 12,1292m (40,000ft) at the southern group of targets – so that the northerly wind would not pull smoke over the northern targets – recording three direct hits. The second flight began its attack with two F-15B/Ds releasing their GBU-15s, one of which scored a direct hit. The mission leader then joined up with two F-15Cs, one of which dropped his Mk.82s on the first run, while the other had to make a circle and re-attack from a different direction because of dense smoke covering the target.

As far as can be assessed from all available sources, this attack was a complete success: the PLO HQ was totally destroyed. Sources differ significantly regarding casualties: while the Israelis claimed that up to 75 people were killed (around 60 of whom were PLO members, including a few from Force 17), others claimed up to 56 Palestinians and 215 Tunisians were killed, and about 100 wounded. Official Tunisian sources put the final count at 47 dead and 65 wounded.[32]

Achille Lauro Affair

While the PLO restrained from exacting revenge, one of its offshoots – the Palestine Liberation Front (PLF) – did not. Working along a plan for a suicide attack on Israeli soldiers in the port of Ashdod, developed over nearly 11 months, four of them hijacked the Italian liner MS *Achille Lauro* off the coast of Egypt on 7 October 1985. After directing the vessel to Tartus in Syria, the hijackers demanded the release of 50 Palestinians detained in Israeli prisons. On 8 October, the Syrian government refused permission for *Achille Lauro* to dock at Tartus: the hijackers then murdered a retired wheelchair-bound Jewish American businessman and forced the ship's barber and waiter to throw his body and wheelchair overboard. Subsequently, the hijackers ordered the ship towards Port Said in Egypt: after two days of negotiations, they agreed to give up in exchange for safe conduct to Tunisia.

Although condemning the Israeli attack on the PLO HQ in Tunisia, President Reagan put the US Navy's SEAL Team Six and the US Army's Delta Force on alert for a possible rescue attempt when *Achille Lauro* was hijacked. F-14 Tomcats and Lockheed S-3A Vikings from the aircraft carrier USS *Saratoga* (CV-60) tracked the liner for two days until it reached Port Said. Subsequently, *Saratoga* was released from her station and departed for a port call at Dubrovnik in Yugoslavia.[33]

However, when it became known that the hijackers had murdered one of the hostages, the White House and Pentagon put all suitable military assets in the Mediterranean Sea on alert on 10 October. The Italians deployed four HH-3F helicopters of the 15th Stormo at Akrotiri in Cyprus, with a team of the Italian navy diver commandos (COMSUBIN). During the day, three Boeing EC-135 and RC-135 ELINT/SIGINT gatherers with Arab linguists on board and one Boeing E-3A Sentry airborne early warning and control system (AWACS) aircraft of the USAF were recorded patrolling off the Egyptian coast. Eventually, US intelligence found out that the Egyptian government decided that a chartered Boeing 737-226 of EgyptAir, registration SU-AYH, would take four hijackers of the *Achille Lauro* and two Palestinians to Tunisia, during the evening of 10 October. The US Commander-in-Chief Europe (USCINCEUR) in Vahingen, West Germany, called the Commander-in-Chief US Naval Forces Europe (CINCUSNAVEUR) in London, and he in turn communicated with the Commander of the USN's 6th Fleet in Gaeta, Italy, and on to the Commander of Saratoga Carrier Battle Group (CVBG), Rear Admiral David E. Jeremiah, embarked on *Saratoga*. On their order, Commander, Carrier Air Wing 17

SS *Achille Lauro* was hijacked while crusing from Alexandria in Egypt to Ashdod in Israel, on 7 October 1985. (Mark Lepko Collection)

USS *Saratoga* (CV-60), an aircraft carrier of Forrestal-class, was to play a prominent role in many of the events in the Mediterranean during late 1985 and early 1986. The ship is shown at full steam, with aircraft of CVW-17 embarked. (US Navy Photo)

The deck of the USS *Saratoga* in late 1985. In the foreground are two F-14A Tomcats from VF-103 'Sluggers', one painted in gull gray overall, the other in the then still new 'tactical camouflage pattern' consisting of three different shades of ghost gray. Behind them is a single A-7E Corsair II from VA-83 'Rampagers', additional Tomcats and several A-6E Intruders from VA-85 'Black Falcons'. (US Navy Photo)

An EA-6B ICAP-II of VAQ-137 – four of which were embarked on USS *Saratoga* in autumn 1985 –about to be launched with the help of a steam catapult. ICAP-II (or 'Block 86') Prowlers were brand new arrivals in the Mediterranean in October 1985. Apart from ALQ-99 ECM-systems, their equipment comprised the powerful ALQ-126 self-protection system (identifiable by saw tooth antennas at the bottom of the refuelling probe and the 'beer can' antenna at the bottom of the tail fin radome). (US Navy Photo)

KA-6D Intruder tankers from squadron VA-85 played a crucial role in supporting other aircraft involved in the interception of the EgyptAir B737. (US Navy Photo)

(CVW-17), Robert 'Bubba' Brodsky developed a plan to intercept the Egyptian airliner, and this was approved by the White House.

Tomcat Surprise

The first Grumman E-2C Hawkeye airborne early warning (AEW) aircraft of the USN's squadron VAW-125 Tigertails was catapulted from *Saratoga* less than an hour from the moment its crew was put on alert, followed by two F-14A Tomcats, around 1845 local time. The second Hawkeye was catapulted around 2130. One of the two E-2Cs took up a position over the Strait of Otranto (the southern entrance into the Adriatic Sea) and acted as a back-up, while the other continued further south. Around 2200, *Saratoga* launched four additional F-14As from VF-74 and VF-103, at least two Grumman EA-6B ICAP-II Prowlers from VAQ-137, two additional KA-6D tankers and one Douglas EA-3B Skywarrior electronic warfare aircraft from VAQ-33 in quick succession. Three further Tomcats followed about an hour later. The southern E-2C, meanwhile, reached a position off the coast of Crete and scanned the sky for any airliners emerging out of Egyptian airspace, while the first two F-14As – supported by one of the KA-6Ds established a barrier combat air patrol (BARCAP) roughly north of Benghazi.

Operating as a team in the darkness of night, the other aircraft launched what was the most sophisticated anti-terror operation ever undertaken until that date, as explained by Sam 'Spoon' Witherspoon, one of the F-14-pilots involved:

Underway in total radio silence, Tomcats occupied four BARCAP stations. Our only communication to the E-2C that controlled the entire operation was via data-link. The Hawkeye from Tigertails

Squadron vectored us from one airliner to the other. I was appointed the southern-most BARCAP-station and intercepted several Il-76s at first, all of which were underway to Libya. Each time I would approach from behind and below, and then my RIO (radar intercept officer) would shortly turn on a flash-light in order to read their registration. Each time we quickly disappeared without being noticed.[34]

The EA-3B and one of the USAF's EC-135s carried Arab linguists who were listening to Egyptian air traffic control. Sometime after 2200 local time, they intercepted a communication between a Boeing 737 of EgyptAir and Tunisian flight control, which indicated that the Tunisians forbade an entry into their airspace. Shortly afterwards, the EA-6Bs jammed all further transmissions from the 737, de-facto isolating the airliner from the outside world.

Meanwhile, the E-2C quickly vectored four F-14As to intercept. The next airliner they found was 'wrong' again, and there was nearly a mid-air collision, but the Americans continued, as Witherspoon explained:

After a while, the Hawkeye ordered us in [a] north-eastern direction, and my WSO to search with radar for a target some 77 miles (124km) away. Shortly after, the Tomcat modex 'AA205' – flown by our CO, 'Skid' Massey, with 'Dog' Cloud as RIO – found the 'right' Boeing 737.

Massey and Cloud intercepted the Egyptian airliner while it was at an altitude of 10,363m (34,000ft), south of the island of Crete. They approached it from the rear and below with their navigational lights turned off and then used a hand-held flashlight to identify it as SU-AYH from a vertical separation of only 4.5m (15ft), while both aircraft were at an airspeed of 740kmph (400 knots). Five other F-14s, the EC-135, the EA-3B and one of the EA-6Bs then joined the emerging 'formation', while the southern E-2C took over all communications with the Boeing using a very high frequency (VHF) radio channel.

Intimidated by the terrorists, the Egyptians initially refused to follow American instructions: the E-2C then ordered all the USN aircraft around the Boeing to move forward of the airliner and turn on their navigation lights, and advised the pilot to land at Naval Air Station (NAS) Sigonella, a major NATO air base on Sicily. The Egyptians attempted to contact Cairo and Tunisia, but without success: their radio remained jammed by the EA-6B. Finally, they gave up and agreed to follow US orders.

The Boeing 737 touched down on the runway of NAS Sigonella at 0015 on 11 October, as three F-14s circled overhead, effectively closing the airspace for all other aircraft – except two Lockheed C-141 StarLifters of the USAF, which carried SEAL Team Six. An additional Tomcat equipped with a TARPS-reconnaissance pod flew overhead to take photographs of the Boeing and two StarLifters on the runways of Sigonella.

Down on the ground, US special forces quickly surrounded the EgyptAir Boeing, but were in turn surrounded by Italian Carabinieri who requested the hijackers to be delivered to them. In the following minutes, tensions increased to a point where soldiers of two allies nearly opened fire at each other.

Italian authorities were meanwhile insistent on getting the hijackers. While the US intercept operation was developing, the US Ambassador to Rome, Maxwell Rabb, attempted in vain to contact Italian Prime Minister Bettino Craxi in order to inform him about

A scene from the combat information centre aboard USS *Saratoga* during the interception of EgyptAir Boeing 737 SU-AYH, on the evening of 10 October 1985. The situation map on the big screen in the background makes it obvious that the carrier was still in the southern Adriatic Sea when this operation was launched. (Albert Grandolini Collection)

This F-14A from VF-103 was the Tomcat that intercepted EgyptAir B737 SU-AYH on the evening of 10 October 1985. (Jean-Marie Lipka)

EgyptAir Boeing 737 SU-AYH on the tarmac of NAS Sigonella, together with one of two C-141 StarLifters that flew in US special forces, on the morning of 11 October 1985. (Albert Grandolini Collection)

what was going on, and to express US insistence on the arrest of the hijackers. Eventually, Colonel Oliver North, who oversaw the entire operation at the Pentagon, was forced to contact Michael Leeden in Maryland, who used to know Craxi personally from the time when he was working at the US Embassy in Rome. Leeden finally managed to make a call to a surprised Craxi, who answered with a question, 'Why Sicily?' The American offered a laconic answer, 'Because there is nowhere in the world a place which combined such beautiful weather, rich cultural heritage and good food.'

Not amused, Craxi immediately made a call to the Director of the SISMI, Admiral Fulvio Martini, and ordered him to enforce Italian sovereignty in Sigonella. That was the reason for the Carabinieri surrounding US special forces that encircled the Egyptian Boeing, almost causing a mutual fire-fight in the process. Even a telephone call from President Reagan, who first attempted to cajole and then threaten Craxi, failed to change the opinion of the Italian Premier: he refused to extradite the hijackers, claiming that because *Achille Lauro* was an Italian ship, they should be put on trial by an Italian tribunal. Around 0400 on 11 October, shortly after Admiral Martini arrived in Sigonella, the Americans finally embarked the two C-141s and flew away.

Table 2: Composition of CVW-17 (USS *Saratoga*), August 1985 – April 1986

Aircraft carrier	Carrier Air Wing & Squadrons	Aircraft type & Modex	Duration of deployment and notes
USS *Saratoga* **(CV-60)**	**CVW-17**	(AA)	25 August 1985 16. April 1986
	VF-74 Be-Devillers	F-14A AA100	
	VF-103 Sluggers	F-14A AA200	
	VA-83 Rampagers	A-7E AA300	
	VA-81 Sunliners	A-7E AA400	
	VA-85 Black Falcons	A-6E & KA-6D AA500	
	VAW-125 Tiger Tails	E-2C AA010	
	VAQ-137 Scorpions	EA-6B AA600	embarked in January 1986
	VS-30 Diamondcutters	S-3A AA700	
	HS-3 Tridents	SH-3H AA730	
	VQ-2 Batmen Det. ?	EA-3B JQ14	embarked in January 1986

Attack of a Sabreliner

While most stories about this interception usually end at this point, the drama surrounding the Egyptian Boeing 737 SU-AYH actually went on. Around 0550 on 11 October, the four hijackers finally emerged out of the aircraft and surrendered to the Carabinieri and the Italian Judge Roberto Pennissi. However, PLF-leader Abu Abbas and PLO representative Hani el-Assan remained on board, together with 17 Egyptian crew and soldiers. After negotiations that lasted for most of the day, and in the light of Egyptian authorities officially requesting the return of the airliner while threatening not to release *Achille Lauro*, which was still docked at Port Said, the decision was taken to let the Boeing 737 return to Cairo.

The airliner took off from Sigonella around 2155, followed by a Piaggio PD.808 carrying Admiral Martini. Suspicious about US intentions, Martini requested a fighter escort – and was soon proven right.

A North American T-39 Sabreliner of the USAF that had remained at Sigonella took off from there around 2204 – without authorisation from the Italian flight control. After a few minutes, it caught up with the airliner carrying the hijackers and began shadowing it from a very close position, apparently calling the crew and trying to divert the Boeing to a USAF base in Spain. Only the arrival of two F-104S Starfighters from the XII Gruppo/26th Stormo, scrambled from Gioia del Colle AB, saved the situation, forcing the Sabreliner away.

The Egyptian pilot meanwhile turned his aircraft east and into Italian airspace, and only then continued north again. Minutes later, the Boeing was joined by a pair of F-104S from the X Gruppo/9th Stormo, scrambled from Grazzanise AB.[35] When this formation of six aircraft approached Rome, it suddenly sighted shadows of two additional unknown fighters approaching through the darkness from the rear. One of the Italian pilots involved later recalled:

It was dark but there was enough residual light to see for a few hundred metres. Two F-14 Tomcats appeared from the rear with their navigational lights out. One passed by me and took a position very close to the Boeing 737. We called them on the radio, several times, warned them, and wiggled with our wings to attract their attention to us: I gave the front Tomcat hand signals to distance. But its pilot reacted with [a] sharp turn to the side and positioned behind our Number 4 Starfighter. As the Number 4 turned to the side, I've heard Number 3 calling, 'This Zombie is still behind you and doing so as if he can't hear us, that idiot!' The other American exploited this confusion and attempted to get close to the Boeing, but I manoeuvred my Starfighter inbetween him and the airliner. He evaded to the side and accelerated. [I'd] had enough, and screamed on the radio in English: 'Get lost before we collide, you piece of shit!'[36]

This time there was an immediate answer from the Americans:

You damn sons of bitches! This aircraft is mine. Do you understand? Mine! Get out of my way!

Meanwhile, all eight aircraft approached within about 40km of Rome and the Egyptian pilot of the Boeing 737 began to descend for landing. Realising the Italian Starfighter pilots would not give up, the two Tomcats descended too; accelerating away at very low altitude, they disappeared under the radar horizon of the Italian flight control – supposedly with the help of electronic countermeasures.

SU-AYH landed safely at Ciampino IAP around 2306 local time. Only seven minutes later, a T-39 Sabreliner – apparently the same that took off from Sigonella and shadowed SU-AYH on the first part of her trip to Rome – appeared over Ciampino, as recalled by the same Italian pilot:

The American demanded permission to land, but his request was turned down. Then he declared [an] emergency and turned off his radio. He landed and rolled towards the Boeing with [no regard] for everybody else, prompting [the] local authorities to temporarily close the airport. Finally, he stopped close to [the] Egyptians but by then Carabinieri were in position: they surrounded the Sabreliner, and the crew was taken way. I don't know what happened to them, but guess that affair was quickly swept under the carpet.

Although US officials presented recordings to Craxi of intercepted radio messages between Abu Abbas and the hijackers while the latter were still onboard *Achille Lauro* on the morning of 12 October, the suspicious Italian Prime Minister declared them

The pilot of EgyptAir B737 SU-AYH, Mohammed Moneib, after arrival in Rome. (Albert Grandolini Collection)

EgyptAir B737 SU-AYH after arrival at Rome IAP, on the night of 11-12 October 1985. (Albert Grandolini Collection)

Three F-14A Tomcats from VF-103 parked on the bow of the *Saratoga* in late 1985. (US Navy photo)

The fin and rear fuselage section of the T-39 Sabreliner that shadowed the EgyptAir Boeing 737 from Sigonella to Rome IAP during the night of 11–12 October 1985. (Albert Grandolini Collection)

The F-14A modex 'AA107' from VF-74, rolling towards one of the bow catapults on the *Saratoga*. During nearly all operations in the Mediterranean in late 1985 and early 1986, Tomcats of this squadron and those from VF-103 were armed with AIM-7 Sparrows and AIM-9 Sidewinders, and carried none of the AIM-54 Phoenix long-range missiles. (US Navy photo)

insufficient to prosecute Abbas and el-Assan. On the contrary, the Boeing 737 was quickly refuelled and transferred to Fiumicino IAP near Rome, where the two Palestinians boarded a Yugoslavian airliner for Belgrade under false names. The EgyptAir airliner was left to return to Cairo, where the pilots received a hero's welcome.

Massacre at Malta

US actions related to hijacking of *Achille Lauro* had negative consequences not only for relations between Rome and

Washington, but for those between USA and Egypt too. This became obvious when the White House, National Security Council and CIA launched a multi-prong strategy against Libya, Operation Flower, later in autumn 1985. Flower had two sub-components, code-named Rose and Tulip. Operation Rose was a plan for an attack on Libya by a US ally, preferably Egypt, which would be supported by the US military, while Operation Tulip was a CIA attempt to overthrow Gaddafi by supporting Libyan exiles, primarily via Egypt. Rose was never realised because Egyptian President Hosni Mubarak refused to invade another Arab country with the assistance of the USA, especially not after what he declared an 'act of piracy' against EgyptAir's Boeing 737. Unsurprisingly, Tulip was exposed to the public soon afterwards by an unknown individual opposed to the plan, and had to be abandoned.[37]

Tragically, all of this was soon forgotten because of the next act of aerial piracy over the Mediterranean.

On 24 November 1985, the very same EgyptAir Boeing 737-266, registration SU-AYH, was hijacked by three gunmen of

Sleek and fast, the 'Zipper' (as the F-104 Starfighter was nicknamed by US pilots) was the backbone of the AMI's interceptor fleet in the 1980s. The aircraft was usually armed with AIM-7E Sparrows and AIM-9B Sidewinders at the time. (Albert Grandolini collection)

the Abu Nidal Palestinian militant group while underway from Athens to Cairo. After the terrorist leader ordered the pilot to fly to Libya, he began checking all passports of the passengers and crew. An Egyptian Security Service agent then attempted to intervene and opened fire, killing one of the gunmen before being wounded along with two flight attendants. The fuselage of the aircraft was punctured too, causing a rapid depressurisation. In emergency, the pilot landed the Boeing at Luqa IAP, although the Maltese authorities refused landing permission and turned off the runway lights. After the Maltese Prime Minister assumed responsibility for the negotiations, the hijackers released 11 passengers and two injured flight attendants. However, because the Maltese refused to refuel the aircraft, the terrorists threatened to kill a passenger every 15 minutes until their demands were met. During the next hour, they shot two Israeli women and three Americans, three of whom survived.

Meanwhile, France, Great Britain and the United States offered to send special forces to help, but the Maltese government feared possible repercussions and accepted Egyptian help instead. Several F-14 Tomcats from USS *Saratoga* patrolled the skies around Malta too, in order to ascertain that there would be no interference by the Libyan air force.

While negotiations were prolonged as much as possible, the Egyptian Task Force 777, a unit of as-Sai'qa ('Thunderbolt') commandos, was flown in, led by four US officers. After a short preparation, the Egyptians attacked without any previous

Despite close military cooperation with the USA, and several joint exercises run during the early 1980s, the Egyptian government refused to become involved in Operation Flower and launch a US-supported invasion of Libya. The F-4E Phantom II interceptors of the Egyptian Air Force – like that shown here – thus never became involved in any combat operations against the western neighbour of Egypt.
(US Navy photo)

warnings, about an hour earlier than agreed with the Maltese authorities. Detonation of explosive devices that ripped open luggage compartment and passenger doors caused a fire inside the aircraft – possibly helped by hand grenades reportedly lobbed by hijackers into the passenger area. The fire and smoke killed 54 of the remaining 87 passengers, two crew members and one hijacker. The terrorist leader escaped during the assault, pretending to be an injured passenger. Egyptian commandos tracked him to St Luke's General Hospital, where he was arrested while trying to take several doctors and medical staff as hostages.

CHAPTER 3
ATTAIN DOCUMENT

White House, along with the National Security Council (NSC), the Pentagon, State Department and various US intelligence services, were still busy discussing Operation Flower, negotiating with the Egyptian government and other allies and considering various other options, when terrorists delivered their next blow. On 27 December 1985, unsuspecting passengers queuing at the check-in counters of airlines such as El Al, TWA and Pan Am at the airports of Rome and Vienna were attacked by gunmen of the Abu Nidal organisation, armed with automatic rifles and hand grenades. The terrorists murdered 20 people – some at close range – and injured more than 70 others. The worldwide shock at the massacre turned into outrage when Libyan news agency JANA declared these attacks as 'heroic operations'. From the standpoint of President Reagan and his administration, and with the availability of questionable circumstantial evidence of Libyan involvement, the perpetrator behind these savage acts was 'obvious' – Libya. While it was soon clear that Syria was its starting point, not only were the air defences of that country much stronger, but US recollections of engaging these – over Lebanon in autumn 1983 – were still very fresh. Syria was already engaged in a 'missile crisis' with Israel, caused by deliveries of long-range S-200VE Vega (ASCC-code SA-5 Gammon) surface-to-air missiles (SAMs) from the Soviet Union. Washington – which used Syria as a starting point for clandestine negotiations with Tehran, related to a number of US and Western hostages held by Hezbollah in Lebanon was not keen to appear overly supportive of Israeli threats against Damascus. Libya, meanwhile, exposed itself to a military counterattack – if not through its own actions, then through statements of its strongman leader, its relative isolation on the international scene and its military weakness. Even once the CIA found out that Gaddafi once deposited US$1 million in Abu Nidal's bank account, Reagan still had to realise that an outright and immediate military action against Tripoli was not viable: the USA had first to exhaust all diplomatic options in an attempt to subdue Libyan support for international terrorism, and then only act in self-defence.

This was the background for the decision of the NSC – presided over by new national security adviser Vice Admiral John M. Poindexter – to start developing a list of military options Reagan could use against Libya. The list ranged from attacks by carrier-borne aircraft of the US Navy to attacks by General Dynamics F-111 fighter-bombers based in Great Britain, strikes by Boeing B-52 Stratofortress bombers based in the continental United States or attacks with the help of air-, ship- or submarine-launched cruise missiles. A contingency list of Libyan targets also came into being, ranging from anti-aircraft sites to terrorist-related facilities and official buildings. Following extensive discussions in the course of two NSC meetings on 6 and 7 January 1986, and in the light of severe concern over the possibility of US servicemen

being captured by Libyans, Secretary of State George Schultz proposed a combination of diplomatic and economic sanctions, and an operation that would be similar yet larger in scope to the earlier 'Freedom of Navigation' (FON) operations in the Gulf of Syrte, run by CVBGs around USS *Forrestal* (CV-59) and USS *Nimitz* (CVN-68) in 1981, USS *Eisenhower* (CVN-69) in 1983 and USS *Saratoga* in 1984. Preferably, all such operations would be undertaken in concert with European allies, but if not, the USA was ready to undertake them alone.

Listening to his military advisers, President Reagan eventually ruled out the use of B-52s and cruise missiles. Repositioning of strategic bombers or deployment of cruise missiles could easily upset the Soviets, who were likely to warn Gaddafi. It would also compromise the sensitive high technology of cruise missiles. Instead, Reagan issued Executive Order 12543 on 7 January, which banned all travel and commercial transactions between the United States and Libya, effective from 1 February, and a day later authorised additional intelligence operations and military deployments, including a new FON mission in the Gulf of Syrte.

War Fever

By the time the White House finally made up its mind about what to do with Libya, US military preparations had already begun. The Pentagon had issued a top-secret warning to all key USAF and USN commands in EUCOM on the evening of 27 December 1985, advising them to prepare feasibility studies for attacks on Libya. One of the first related decisions was to create a multi-carrier task force in the central Mediterranean. For this purpose, the *Saratoga* was to be reinforced by the carrier battle group centred around USS *Coral Sea* (CV-43) and then by USS *America* (CV-66).

A ship of Midway-class commissioned for service on 1 October 1947, the *Coral Sea* was slightly smaller than the other 15 'super carriers' in service with the USN at the time, but completely rebuilt and expanded, including the addition of an angled deck, relocation of her elevators to the deck edge, installation of three new steam catapults, addition of an enclosed hurricane bow and hull blisters. On this aircraft carrier was Carrier Air Wing 13 (CVW-13). Established on 1 March 1984, this wing had a unique composition: instead of comprising the usual two squadrons of F-14 Tomcats, two squadrons of Ling-Temco-Vought A-7 Corsair IIs and one of A-6 Intruders (in addition to support units flying EA-6Bs, E-2Cs, S-3s and anti-submarine helicopters), it had four squadrons of brand-new McDonnell Douglas F/A-18A Hornet fighter-bombers and one each of A-6 Intruders and E-2C Hawkeyes.[38]

The *Coral Sea* had been in the Mediterranean since 13 October 1985, but through the following month was busy with a series of exercises with the British and French navies and the Turkish air force. Therefore, when put on notice for operations off Libya, CVW-

13 requested reinforcements in the form of a squadron of EA-6Bs. The USN decided to deploy Prowlers of VAQ-135 – a unit that had just completed a work-up period in preparation for deployment on board USS *America*, scheduled to start in February 1986. For this purpose, VAQ-135 was equipped with the seven 'best' jets from different units of the Prowler-wing based at NAS Whidbey Island. They deployed to the Mediterranean during a two-day-long trip via NAS Oceana and Sigonella, with support from tanker aircraft and multiple in-flight refuelling, in early January 1986. Dave 'Hey Joe' Parsons, then a F-14-WSO with squadron VF-102, a part of Carrier Air Wing 1 (CVW-1) embarked on USS *America*, recalled:

> It was a mad rush. VAQ-135 was from our wing, CVW-1, and we [had] just returned from exercise Ocean Safari '85, off Norway. We were doing work-ups for a spring 1986 cruise, when we were told to return to Norfolk and get all the jets ready for war. VAQ-135 was sent right away for *Coral Sea*. They replaced most of [the] engines and swept the jets and got all the parts we could never get, to get every jet in tip-top shape. EA-6Bs of US Marines squadron VMAQ-2 then showed up to replace the VAQ-135 when we deployed. Our squadron underwent a similar process: we got new engines for our F-14s, new radar homing and warning gear and other stuff. I was actually scheduled to leave VF-102 after five years, but was put on 'Op Hold' – which I didn't protest at all because it was obvious Reagan was going to let us cross the so-called 'Line of Death' and do whatever it took to get Gaddafi's attention. VMAQ-2 was pretty colourful at [the] back end of our boat. They were super folks and knew their trade. They helped immeasurably setting up electronic order of battle for our anti-radar missile shooters from A-7 squadrons, later on … It was obvious that big-time saber[sic]-rattling was ahead.

Another aircraft to reinforce CVW-13 was one EA-3B Skywarrior from the USN's squadron VQ-2. Originally designed as a bomber to carry big early nuclear bombs into attacks on the USSR, this old aircraft was modified to serve as an ELINT/SIGINT gatherer and could alternatively serve as a tanker.

Overall, the configuration of CVW-13 was therefore 'pioneering' because – though this was neither known at the time, nor actually intended – 20 years later, and as a consequence of phasing out the F-14s, all the USN's carrier air wings were to become composed in the same fashion, with four squadrons of Hornets and a particularly strong electronic warfare component.

The *Coral Sea* CVBG, commanded by Rear Admiral Jerry C. Breast, rendezvoused with the *Saratoga* CVBG, commanded by Rear Admiral David E. Jeremiah, on 15 January 1986, creating Task Force 60 (TF-60) under Jermiah's command. The task of TF-60 was to run Operation Attain Document with the aim of reaffirming the right of US ships and aircraft to operate in the waters and airspace over the Gulf of Syrte and within the area of responsibility of Tripoli air control, and thus demonstrate US resolve in the struggle against terrorism.

Developed by the commander of the US 6th Fleet, Vice Admiral Frank B. Kelso, Operation Attain Document was carefully designed to satisfy the 'hawks' and 'doves' in Washington. It offered an opportunity of a military confrontation with Libya through deploying combat aircraft and warships ever deeper into the Gulf of Syrte, but did so in a slow and incremental fashion. The Rules of Engagement (RoEs) for USN pilots and officers were similar to those from August 1981, but Kelso went a step further and granted Jeremiah the authority to designate selected Libyan forces as 'hostile' if they exhibited the imminent use of force or if tactical circumstances warranted a vigorous reaction. In essence, this meant that the commanders, pilots and surface operators of TF-60 could exercise self-defence without consulting a higher authority.

Table 3: Composition of CVW-13 (USS *Coral Sea*), October 1985 – May 1986

Aircraft Carrier	Carrier Air Wing & Squadrons	Aircraft Type & Modex	Duration of Deployment & Notes
USS *Coral Sea* (CV-43)	**CVW-13**	(AK)	1 October 1985 19 May 1986
	VFA-131 Wildcats	F/A-18A AK100	
	VFA-132 Privateers	F/A-18A AK200	
	VMFA-314 Black Knights	F/A-18A AK300	
	VMFA-323 Death Rattlers	F/A-18A AK400	
	VA-55 Sea Horses	A-6E & KA-6D AK500	
	VAW-127 Tigertails	E-2C AK600	
	VAQ-135 Black Ravens	EA-6B AK620	embarked 9 January 1986
	HS-17 Neptune's Riders	SH-3H AK	
	VQ-2 Batmen	EA-3B AK	embarked January 1986

Attain Document I

Libyan reaction to the Pentagon's announcement on 24 January of 'routine peacetime naval exercises' within the airspace controlled by flight control in Tripoli was as reserved as expected. Gaddafi put his military on alert and organised another show for selected press, promising war and blood to anybody who attacked Libya. When Attain Document I commenced on 26 January 1986, two brand-new MiG-25PDSs from No. 1035 Squadron approached a pair of F/A-18As from US Marines squadron VMFA-323 (one of four units equipped with the type and embarked on USS *Coral Sea*) on a CAP south of TF-60. Vectored by an E-2C, Hornets circumnavigated around the approaching MiGs and then took position behind the two Libyans. After being tailed by the Americans for nearly 10 minutes, both MiG-25s broke off and returned to base.

For the following four days, USN aircraft continued their operations within the Tripoli Flight Information Region (FIR) almost undisrupted by the LAAF: only eight Libyan interceptors appeared to inspect them, all were easily intercepted, none attempted any air combat manoeuvring and the impressions of the few American pilots who encountered them was that they had poor flight discipline, poor look-around doctrine and were not aggressive.[39] In fact, USN carriers remained well away from

USS *Coral Sea* was the centrepiece of the second CVBG sent to the central Mediterranean to bolster USS *Saratoga* in early 1986. (US Navy photo)

The commander of *Saratoga* CVBG and then TF-60, Rear Admiral David E. Jeremiah, in the combat information centre of the *Saratoga* during operations against Libya in early 1986. (US Navy photo)

USS *Saratoga* (foreground) and USS *Coral Sea* (background) in the central Mediterranean in January 1986. Together, the two aircraft carriers had about 170 combat and combat-support aircraft embarked. (US Navy photo)

An EA-6B Prowler from VQ-135 'Black Ravens' in the process of repositioning on the deck of USS *Coral Sea*, prior to the next launch cycle. The unit was rushed to join CVW-15 in early January 1986. (US Navy photo)

Libya, and none of the F-14As from *Saratoga* and F/A-18As from *Coral Sea* crossed the 'Line of Death' to enter the airspace Libyans claimed as their own.

As usual, interceptors were supported by E-2C Hawkeye AEW aircraft, EA-6B Prowlers and KA-6D Intruder tankers, but their primary concerns appear to have been the issue of operating in the area and learning all the related procedures. Robert E. Stumpf, then the CO of VFA-132 embarked on *Coral Sea*, recalled:

> The *Coral Sea* launched her fighters first on a normal cycle. They would buster [the command given to naval aviators to proceed at best possible speed] to station to relieve the off-going CAP, who would buster back to make the last part of the carrier's recovery cycle. This 300-plus mile transition often took 40 minutes or more during which the ship steamed into the wind, which delayed the re-spot for the next launch and thus decreased time allotted for aircraft refuelling and maintenance.

Although tensions thus remained low, USN pilots remained alert and maintained discipline, as Stumpf commented:

> US pilots flew CAP missions as through their lives depended on it. They practiced non-tactical aspects of maintaining the barrier – such as relieving on station, data-link coordination with the E-2C radar control aircraft, and tanking – until they became routine.

After four days of testing the Libyans, Attain Document I was concluded and TF-60 withdrew further north.

Attain Document II

Just two weeks later, the USN returned to the Gulf of Syrte to run another FON exercise, Operation Attain Document II. Commencing on 12 February, this four-day exercise was to see Americans approaching close to, but not crossing the 'Line of Death'. USN commanders aimed to expose their pilots to genuine MiGs, to 'enemy equipment' they had been studying for years. They began practicing a number of advanced tactical manoeuvres and studied Libyan reactions to these. Like before, F-14s and F/A-18s armed with AIM-7 Sparrows and AIM-9 Sidewinders, and their internal 20mm calibre cannons, acted as primary interceptors. They were ably supported by E-2Cs, which usually detected LAAF fighters as soon as they became airborne – at least when they entered the airspace over the Mediterranean Sea. The capabilities of E-2Cs offered large advantages to Tomcat and Hornet pilots, enabling them to outflank most of the Libyans and approach from the rear of their opponents on nearly every intercept.

As well as combat air patrols (CAPs), F/A-18As, A-6Es and A-7Es – armed with AGM-84A Harpoon anti-ship missiles, Mk.20 Rockeye cluster bomb units (CBUs) and AIM-9 Sidewinders – flew surface combat air patrols (SUCAPs) and actively searched for Libyan warships. Each carrier conducted 13 hours of flight operations each day, and maintained an alert status when not operating over the Gulf of Syrte.

Contrary to Attain Document I, the LAAF reacted in very vivid and often aggressive fashion during Attain Document II. No less than 140 MiG-25s, MiG-23s, Su-22s, Mirage 5s and Mirage F.1 were intercepted in four days of this operation. The flying

The most powerful addition to the LAAF arsenal of the early 1980s was the MiG-25PDS. Powered by improved Tumansky R-15 engines and equipped with N-005 Saphir-25 radar (which had a limited look-down/shoot-down capability), an IRST and R-60MK short-range AAMs, it was a significant improvement over the earlier MiG-25P. Around a dozen were operated by the Mitiga-based No. 1035 Squadron, LAAF, part of which was forward deployed at Ghurdabiyah/Syrte AB, in February March 1986. The insets show details of the MiG-25PDS's main armament, including R-40TD (left) and R-40RD (centre) air-to-air missiles. (Tom Cooper)

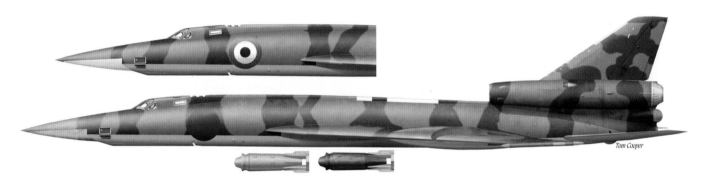

The most powerful offensive weapon in the LAAF arsenal of the 1980s were Tupolev Tu-22 bombers, 14 of which entered service with the al-Jufra/Hun-based Bomber Squadron in 1977. All were camouflaged in colours shown here, in olive green and dark green (exact shades remain unknown) on top surfaces and sides, while undersides were left in natural metal. National insignia was applied in six positions: until 1977, it consisted of the pan-Arabic tricolore (see upper inset), and later of the Libyan green markings. None of the aircraft is known to have worn any kind of usual serials, but it is possible that the last two of their construction number were applied on the cover for the front undercarriage bay. The insets at the bttom of the profile show the usual colours of FAB-1500 bombs (1,500kg calibre), which represented the main weapon of this type in Libyan service. (Tom Cooper)

An Aeritalia F-104S from the Birgi-based XVIII Gruppo (18th Gruppo), 37th Stormo in late 1985 or early 1986. All of these Starfighters were painted in the same camouflage pattern, consisting of colours named Italian dark grey (FS36152) and Italian Dark Green (FS36364) on upper surfaces and sides. Lower surfaces were painted in Italian Medium Grey (FS35526). Some of the 37th Stormo's Starfighters also used to wear the 'Ace of Stick' insignia on their fins, but this was declared 'politically incorrect' (because of its relation with fascism in the 1930s) and therefore removed in early 1985. The primary armament consisted of AIM-7E Sparrows and AIM-9B Sidewinders during the mid-1980s. (Tom Cooper)

The Jaguar A c/n A99, coded 11-MQ, was officially assigned to the EC 2/11 'Vosges' (insignia shown in the inset). During an attack on Wadi Doum AB on 16 February 1986, it was flown by Lieutenant Balandras while in this configuration, carrying 18 BAP-100 runway-cratering bombs on a 30-6-M2 adaptor under the centreline, two RP.35 drop tanks on inboard underwing pylons, a Barracuda ECM-pod on the outboard left pylon and (not shown here) Phimat chaff & flare dispenser on the outboard right pylon. Notable during the operation was the quite fresh coat of tactical camouflage colours, including Brun Café and Brun Noisette. (Tom Cooper)

The Jaguar A c/n A91, coded 11-YG, was officially assigned to EC 4/11 'Yura' (insignia shown in insets). During the attack on Wadi Doum AB it was flown by Captain Delcourt as 'tail-end Charlie' – the rear-most aircraft in a formation – and armed with SAMP 250 bombs (250kg calibre), as shown here. It received 10 hits by bomb splinters from weapons dropped by other aircraft. A91 was repaired at Bangui IAP and returned to service: in 1991, it suffered damage from Iraqi ground fire, thus becoming the only AdA fighter-bomber ever to be damaged twice in two different wars, and always return safely back to base. (Tom Cooper)

The Mirage IVA c/n 31, coded 'BD', was the aircraft of Commandants Jacky Morel and Jules Mérouze during Operation Tobus, on 18 February 1986. Prior to that highly sensitive reconnaissance mission, all external markings and serials were overpainted in order to deny any means of recognition. As well as the usual RP.20 drop tanks (released over northern Sudan and not shown here), the aircraft carried only the giant CT.52 reconnaissance pod installed under the centreline (with the upper part of this pod being inside the aircraft) and a full load of chaff & flares for ALKAN dispensers installed in the bottom of the rear fuselage (not visible from this aspect). As usual for all Mirage IVs before the 1990s, it was camouflaged in blue grey (FS35164) overall and dark green grey on upper surfaces and sides, but wore no unit insignia. Inset is the crest of ERI 1/328. (Tom Cooper)

The F-14A modex AB200 (tailcode was applied on insides of both rudders only) – BuAerNo 161142 – wore the so-called 'CAG-markings' during VF-33's cruise on USS America in 1986. Painted in Gull Gray overall (FS16440), the aircraft is shown in configuration as flown during the clash with a pair of Libyan MiG-25s on 24 March 1986: with TCS under the front fuselage, and two each of AIM-54A Phoenix, AIM-7F Sparrow and AIM-9L Sidewinder AAMs. (Tom Cooper)

Like many other F-14As of that unit, the VF-102's Tomcat with modex AB110 was painted in gull gray overall and wore not only the usual row of 'diamonds' applied in a dull red colour down the forward fuselage but also further traditional insignia on wing gloves, drop tanks and fins. Crews of this squadron preferred to have their F-14s loaded lightly, and thus usually had them armed with four each of AIM-7F or AIM-7M Sparrows and AIM-9L Sidewinders. (Tom Cooper)

The A-6E modex AB510 – BuAerNo 152948 – is one of the few Intruders positively identified as operated by the VA-34 'Blue Blasters' squadron during Operation Prairie Fire in March 1986. It was painted in the lighter version of the tactical camouflage pattern, consisting of gray FS36231 on top surfaces and sides and FS36320 on undersurfaces, and is shown armed with one AGM-84A Harpoon installed (as usual) on the left inboard underwing pylon. (Tom Cooper)

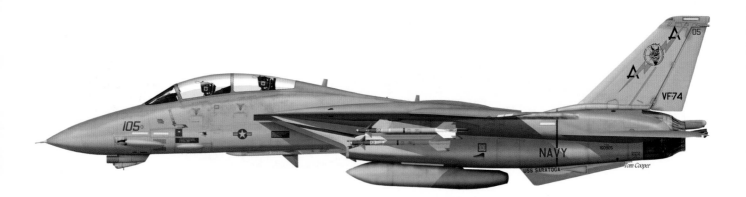

A reconstruction of the F-14A modex AA105 – BuAerNo 160905 – in the colours of VF-74 during the Mediterranean cruise of 1985 1986. The aircraft was painted in a standardised tactical paint scheme (TPS) consisting of Dark Ghost Gray (FS36320) over Light Ghost Gray (FS36375). Uniquely for Tomcats of CVW-17 in 1984, all top surfaces and areas around the cockpit were further camouflaged with dark grey (FS 35237). (Tom Cooper)

A reconstruction of the F-14A modex AA205 – BuAerNo 160904 – the crew of which intercepted and positively identified the EgyptAir B737 SU-AYH on 10 October 1985. Like most Tomcats from VF-103, this F-14A received not only the standardised TPS consisting of Dark Ghost Gray (FS36320) over Light Ghost Gray (FS36375), but also the much darker FS35237 on all top surfaces. As far as is known, the armament during that mission consisted of six AIM-7 Sparrows and two AIM-9 Sidewinders. (Tom Cooper)

All the A-6E Intruders of VA-85 wore the standardised TPS consisting of Dark Ghost Gray (FS36320) over Light Ghost Gray (FS36375) in 1986, which suffered heavily from the effects of Mediterranean weather in January and February of that year, but also intensive flying during Operations Attain Document I/II/III. This example wears two kill markings for Libyan warships sunk during the night of 24 to 25 March 1986 and is armed with a pair of Mk. 20 Rockeye CBUs. (Tom Cooper)

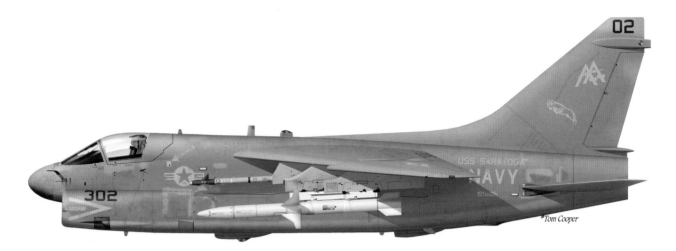

Like other tactical combat aircraft of the USN, most A-7Es were painted in the TPS, consisting of Dark Ghost Gray (FS36320) on upper surfaces and sides, over Light Ghost Gray (FS36375) on undersurfaces. Due to the high tempo of operations in January and February 1986, most aircraft began showing rather well-worn colours, often touched up by quick bursts of spray paint to prevent corrosion. Wearing the markings of VA-83 'Rampagers', this example is illustrated armed with an AGM-88A HARM and an AIM-9L Sidewinder. (Tom Cooper)

Even more worn out was the paintwork of the A-7E with modex AA401, the bird usually assigned to the Squadron CO of VA-81 'Sunliners' – the second light attack squadron assigned to USS Saratoga during the Mediterranean cruise of 1985 1986. The aircraft is illustrated armed with a pair of Mk. 20 Rockeye CBUs: while Corsairs did not deploy any of these during Prairie Fire, they did fly plenty of SUCAPs in such configuration. (Tom Cooper)

A reconstruction of the A-6E modex AK501, assigned to the CO VA-55 'Sea Horses'. This relatively short-lived unit was established with the purpose of providing an Intruder-equipped unit to the then still new CVW-15, when this was preparing to embark on USS Coral Sea in 1984. The squadron saw much action during Prairie Fire, when its A-6Es were involved in the sinking of at least one Libyan warship (note a small black kill marking underneath the cockpit). AK501 is illustrated in one of the weapons configurations that was the result of experiences from operations off Libya, including an AGM-84A Harpoon anti-ship missile on inboard pylon and an AIM-9L Sidewinder on the outboard pylon. (Tom Cooper)

Painted in the weathered tactical camouflage pattern consisting of Dark Ghost Gray (FS36320) over Light Ghost Gray (FS36375), F/A-18As from US Marine Corps' VMFA-314 'Black Knights' squadron showed relatively little in terms of insignia during the 1985–1986 cruise on board USS Coral Sea. The single exception was the traditional fashion of applying that unit's designation on the sides of the centre fuselage. (Tom Cooper)

The second Marine Fighter Attack Squadron embarked on USS Coral Sea was VMFA-323 'Death Rattlers'. Like the aircraft of VMFA- 314, its Hornets wore a minimum of insignia, including the usual modex, unit designation and ship name. Most of the markings should have been applied in dark blue (FS35237). (Tom Cooper)

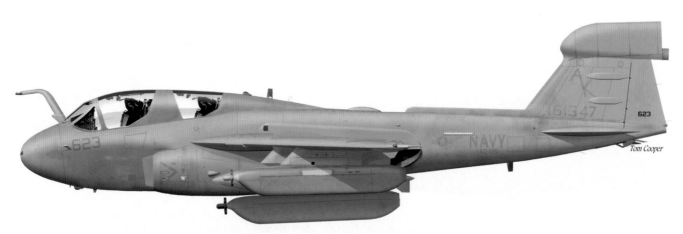

With the VAQ-135 being rushed to USS Coral Sea on 1 January 1986, its crews had little time for applying any other kind of unit insignia on their aircraft, except for the tailcode 'AK'. Something similar can be said about their camouflage pattern, which consisted of Dark Ghost Gray (FS36320) on top surfaces and sides, over Light Ghost Gray (FS 36375). While the few available photographs are rather unclear in this regards, it seems that AK623 received an additional touch of some other colour than the usual dark gray FS35237 around the cockpit. (Tom Cooper)

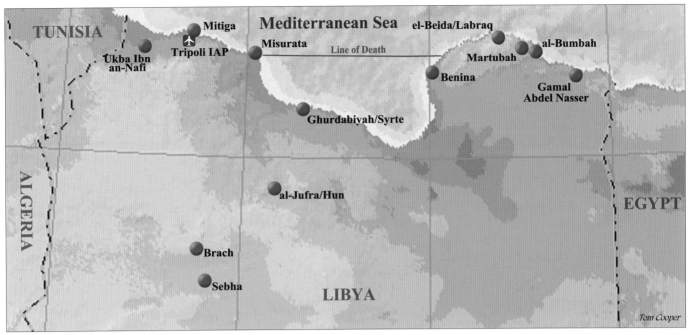

Map of major air bases in northern and central Libya in the mid-1980s. (Map by Tom Cooper)

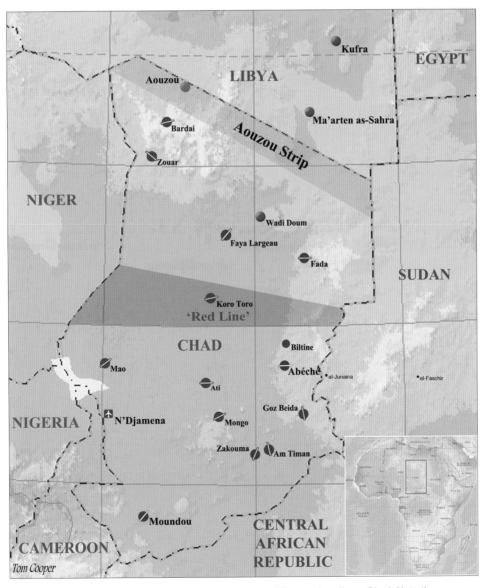

Map of airfields in Chad and LAAF air bases in southern Libya and northern Chad. Note the dominant position of Wadi Doum AB. (Map by Tom Cooper)

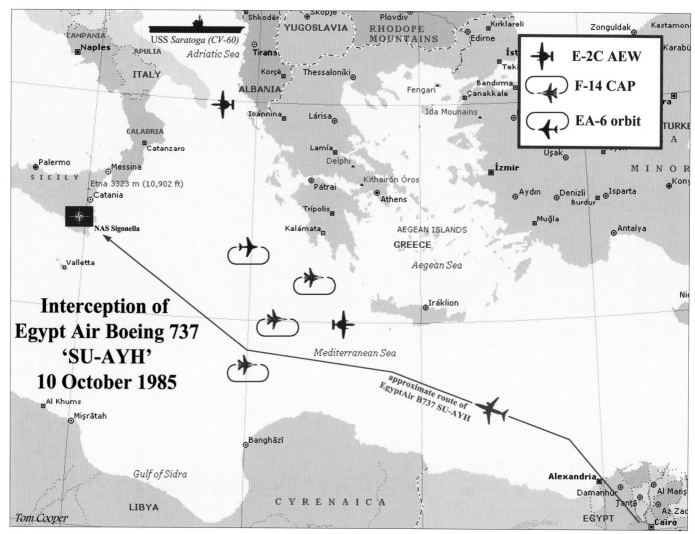

Map of the interception of EgyptAir Boeing 737 SU-AYH, during the night of 10 to 11 October 1985. (Map by Tom Cooper)

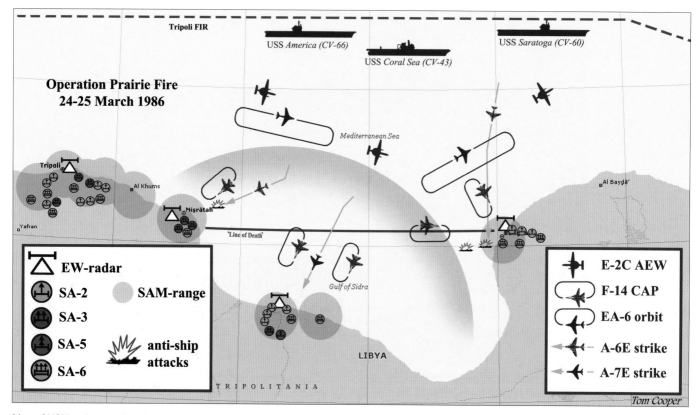

Map of USN actions and major Libyan SAM-sites during Operation Prairie Fire on 24 and 25 March 1986. (Map by Tom Cooper)

became so intensive that even crews of KA-6D tankers got their opportunity to encounter Libyan MiGs, while 'pure' bombers like A-6E Intruders were also armed with AIM-9 Sidewinders for self-defence. Stumpf attempted to explain this in the following fashion:

This aggressive Libyan response may have been due to emphasis from Soviet advisers to demonstrate existing capabilities. Also, the Libyans may have perceived a hostile intent during [Attain Document] I, but felt more confident after [USN] forces withdrew without challenging their claim to the Gulf of Syrte.

Recollections of Libyan pilots do not cite any influence of Soviet advisers. Rather, the LAAF simply reacted to more vivid activity of greater numbers of USN aircraft closer to what it considered the borders of sovereign Libyan airspace.

Generally, USN pilots were rather unimpressed by the skills of their Libyan opponents. Although the LAAF GCI operators regularly provided accurate vectors to the American CAP stations, USN pilots regularly outmatched their opponents once the intercept phase of engagement began. According to Stumpf:

...[Some] appeared to slide down in the cockpit as through they could keep from being shot by not exposing their upper torso through the canopy.

According to former LAAF pilots, their problems were of an entirely different nature – and once again related not only to US technology outmatching the Soviet equipment in their hands, but also to the rather poor work of their GCI controllers. Abdoul Hassan, former MiG-23-pilot, explained:

It was the same like in 1981. We would receive the order to look for one target, flew there – and found nothing. Then two F-14s would appear behind us. Although Soviets told us the MiG-23 could outturn the F-14 at [a] certain speed, this proved impossible. We could not outmanoeuvre them and decided to return to our base ... We depended on the GCI, but our ground controllers were not good. With most of [the] engagements taking place well away from our coast, our GCI always needed 10-15 seconds to react to every American move. At a speed of 500knots, we were travelling over 50km in less than three minutes, approaching our American opponents at a combined speed in excess of Mach 1.5 – all the time distancing ever further away from our ground radars. This meant that the reaction time of our GCI was getting ever longer the more the distance to [the] Americans decreased. Nearly always the GCI ordered us to activate our radars much too late, when we were less than 10km from [the] Americans. By that time, Tomcats were already manoeuvring around us, achieving positions of advantage.

MiG-23 pilots from Benina AB near Benghazi appear to have borne the brunt of LAAF operations during Attain Document II, and – according to the Americans – proved the most aggressive. Some made attempts to shake the Hornets and Tomcats off their tails, others flew hard oblique weaves, accelerated to supersonic

speeds or decelerated to very slow airspeeds. XY's recollection confirmed this indirectly:

In one case I was scrambled to intercept two American aircraft operating inside our airspace. As I was approaching my target, I passed two MiG-23s that were returning from a similar mission and their leader informed me about [the] presence of two Tomcats. [A] minute later I briefly saw the Americans and manoeuvred to intercept but it was an ambush: two others appeared behind me.

Apparently unknown to the USN at the time, one of two MiG-23-squadrons based at Benina in 1986 was exclusively manned by Syrian pilots. While the official USN version is that not one

An E-2C Hawkeye of VAW-127 'Tigertails' squadron preparing for catapult-assisted take-off from USS *Coral Sea* in January 1986. This airborne early warning aircraft was the centrepiece of all the US Navy's operations off Libya. (US Navy photo)

Libyan MiG-25PDS serial number 7029 being shadowed by an F/A-18A Hornet from VMFA-314 'Black Knights' on the morning of 26 January 1986. Despite their longer-ranged radar and superior speed, both MiGs were easily outflanked by USN fighters and tailed for nearly 10 minutes. (US Navy photo)

The other MiG-25PDS from No. 1035 Squadron, LAAF, intercepted by Hornets on the same morning, was this aircraft, serial number 6716. (US Navy photo)

Top: A bottom view of the same MiG-25PDS, revealing details of its armament – consisting of R-40RD ('AA-6 Acrid'; semi-active-radar homing, medium-range air-to-air missile) and R-60MK (AA-8 Aphid; infra-red homing, short-range air-to-air missile). (US Navy photo)

Middle: F/A-18A Hornet modex AK100 from VFA-131 during catapult launch from USS *Coral Sea* in early 1986. Operations Attain Document I and II were the first operational deployments for this prolific type. (US Navy photo)

F-14A Tomcat modex AA100 during re-spotting prior to catapult-launch from USS *Saratoga* in February 1986. In a rare exception from the rules of the time, and probably because of vivid activity of Libyan MiG-25s, this aircraft was armed not only with AIM-7F Sparrows and AIM-9L Sidewinders (foreground, left), but also with AIM-54 Phoenix long-range missiles (the front part of one is visible between the Sparrow and the drop tank). (US Navy photo)

A beautiful study of the LAAF MiG-23MS serial number 4711, high above the Gulf of Syrte, in February 1986. The aircraft was probably Syrian-flown, and operated by either No. 1040 or No. 1050 Squadron, both of which were based at Benina AB near Benghazi. It was still armed with hopelessly obsolete R-3S (AA-2 Atoll) air-to-air missiles. (US Navy photo)

A Hornet from VFA-131 – flown by USAF exchange pilot Major D. R. 'Doc' Zoerb, tailing a MiG-23MS, serial number 4714, during Operation Attain Document II in February 1986. (US Navy Photo)

Operation Attain Document II saw very intensive flying activity by both sides, sometimes resulting in unexpected encounters. In this case, a LAAF Su-22M-3K fighter-bomber (serial number 1509) armed with R-13M air-to-air missiles and acting as an interceptor was intercepted by an F/A-18A from VFA-132, armed with Sparrows, Sidewinders and Rockeye CBUs – and actually underway on a SUCAP. (US Navy photo)

of the Libyan interceptors achieved a firing position behind an American fighter during Attain Document I and II, it seems that more experienced Syrian pilots were slightly more successful than their Libyan colleagues, and also more successful than the Americans were ready to admit. At least one of them documented an 'air combat' with F-14s that ended with him taking gun-camera photographs of a USN Tomcat.

Much faster MiG-25s certainly remained a problem for the USN, as recalled by Ali Thani:

Our commanders were concerned about [the] possibility of American warships crossing the Line of Death unobserved. We had no AWACS so the idea was born to use Il-76 transports to track down the USN carriers. They usually flew north of Tripoli on an east-west pattern, and were frequently intercepted by Hornets and Tomcats, by day and by night … In one instance we exploited [the] American preoccupation with our Il-76. The crew of the transport advised us

about USN warships they could track with radar. I was scrambled with my wingman and we were intercepted by a pair of Hornets. But, we easily out accelerated the Americans and passed high above one of their carriers, signalling them that they can't hide from us.[40]

In another instance, two MiG-25s reached the EA-3B from USS *Coral Sea* before any of the Tomcats and Hornets patrolling nearby could do so. The Libyans came very close and then passed underneath the reconnaissance aircraft, although without opening fire: the USN's aircraft was outside the airspace claimed by Libya.

By the fourth day of Attain Document II, flying by both sides reached its peak, as recalled by Stumpf:

Taking a vector off the catapult, alert pilots often found themselves intercepting inbound MiGs quite soon after launch, while still completing combat checks and coordinating with the E-2C. In this multiple target arena, correlation between E-2C contacts and on-board radar contacts was essential to ensure that the object of the intercept was truly an adversary and not another USN fighter.

Some of the operations undertaken by the Libyans became quite

Another view of the bottom side of the MiG-25PDS serial 6716. Notable is the armament consisting of 'only' one R-40RD (left) and one R-40TD (infra-red homing variant), but also two pairs of R-60MK short-range AAMs under outboard pylons. (US Navy photo)

An LAAF MiG-25PDS (serial number 7003) intercepted at high altitude by *Saratoga*'s Tomcats while attempting to overfly the centre of TF-60. (US Navy photo)

A good profile-shot of an F/A-18A from VFA-132 'Privateers', in flight along the Libyan-declared 'Line of Death' in February 1986. As usual, the aircraft was armed only with AIM-7 Sparrows (installed on lower sides of engine nacelles) and AIM-9 Sidewinders (on wing-tips). (US Navy photo)

Released recently by the relative of one of the SyAAF pilots who used to serve in Libya in the mid-1980s, this photograph shows the pilot in question (his name remains unknown) together with a LAAF MiG-23MS serial number 8705, at Benina AB (outside Benghazi) in 1985 or 1986. (via Pit Weinert)

Gun-camera picture taken by unknown SyAAF pilot while flying a LAAF MiG-23MS on February 1986, apparently of an F-14A Tomcat interceptor of the US Navy. While the identity of the aircraft in crosshairs cannot be definitely confirmed, and provided this was really one of the USN's Tomcats, this photograph would indicate that not all the MiG-23-formations intercepted by US fighters on this day were as easily outmanoeuvred as usually described by American naval pilots. (via Pit Weinert)

Lacking airborne early warning capability, the LAAF had the idea to utilise navigational radars of their Il-76 transports to find and track USN aircraft carriers. The appearance of these big aircraft attracted lots of attention from US pilots: this example was intercepted by an F/A-18A Hornet from VMFA-323 (unit from the US Marines Corps). (US Navy photo)

The US Operation Attain Document II attracted considerable attention from the Soviets, who began sending their maritime patrol aircraft to shadow the movement of USN aircraft and warships. In this case, an Ilyushin Il-18 was intercepted by an F/A-18A from VFMA-323, high above the Mediterranean Sea. (US Navy photo)

complex, as Abdoul Hassan concluded:

> We attempted to lure Tomcats south of the Line of Death, then to surprise them and establish numerical superiority in the engagement zone. Our aim was to deploy six widely separated MiG-23s to isolate a pair of Tomcats underway inside Libyan airspace. It didn't work: Americans deployed strong jamming, our GCI got confused and our fuel reserves proved insufficient.

In the course of such LAAF operations, F/A-18A Hornets proved particularly valuable. Although CVW-13 held on average only 22 of its 48 Hornets at readiness on the deck of USS *Coral Sea*, the rule was for all of them to be available for immediate use. This was quite unusual for the USN, which had great experience with frequent malfunctions on older aircraft types. Furthermore, while the much more complex F-14 Tomcats proved to work better and suffer less technical issues if flown intensively, Hornets still required nearly 50 percent less maintenance. Thanks to their very advanced Hughes APG-65 radars, F/A-18s proved more versatile too: while the USN limited its F-14As to a single role only, even when armed with Rockeye CBUs and operating as a part of SUCAP, Hornets could easily be re-tasked and deployed as interceptors instead. While less powerful than the mighty but older AWG-9 of the Tomcat, the APG-65 proved capable of detecting LAAF fighters out to a range of 74km while tracking 10 targets at the same time, and it experienced a much lower failure rate than expected.

Satisfied with the results of the exercise, and the immense value of collected intelligence about the Libyans, their equipment and capabilities, Rear Admiral Jeremiah concluded Operation Attain Document II on 15 February and the two CVBGs distanced towards the north.

While many of the involved crews were to enjoy a few days of vacation in various Mediterranean ports during the following days, their commanders almost immediately began the planning for Operation Attain Document III: next time, the USN intended to return to the Libyan coast with a task force consisting of three carrier battle groups.

CHAPTER 4
OPERATION *ÈPERVIER*

Following withdrawal of the French contingent deployed during Opération Manta in late 1984, Chad was de-facto a country split into three parts. The northernmost of these, the uranium-rich Aouzou Strip, was occupied by Libyan troops and annexed by Tripoli in 1973. The vast expanse of Sahara Desert south of Aouzou and down to the 16th Parallel (the so-called 'Red Line') was controlled by Libyan-supported forces of the Transitional National Government (Gouvernment d'Union Nationale de Transition, GUNT), led by Goukouni Oueddei. Chad south of the 16th Parallel was under the control of the official Chadian government, led by Hissène Habré, and his armed forces designated the National Armed Forces of Chad (Forces Armées Nationales du Tchad, FANT).

Although withdrawing from Chad, the French carefully monitored the military build-up of the GUNT with the help of reconnaissance aircraft, but also that of Libyan armed forces in northern Chad during 1985. Photographs and electronic emissions collected by Dassault Mirage IV reconnaissance bombers involved in operations such as Brama, Retine, Tégénaire and Musaraigne, and other kinds of intelligence collected from sources on the ground in Chad and Libya, had shown that Gaddafi was about to strike south again, in early 1986.[41]

The exact reasons for the Libyan decision to restart the war in Chad at that time remain unknown. Its timing was unorthodox, as it took place when Libya was under economic sanctions from the USA, isolated in Africa and the Arab world, and facing a direct military confrontation with the US Navy. It is possible that the decision was related to an attempt to distract US attention away from the Mediterranean, but at least as likely that Gaddafi was forced into action because of infighting within the ranks of his Chadian allies. Whatever the case, when the Libyan attack came, the French and Habré were much better prepared than the Libyans expected: their reactions were quick and decisive.

Libyans and the GUNT

Smarting over defeats his troops experienced during battles in 1983 and 1984, and mimicking a withdrawal, the Libyans scattered and attempted to conceal their troops in the desert of northern Chad for most of 1985 – although without much success, as Habré and Paris were perfectly aware of their continual presence.

For much of 1985, Libya invested heavily in intensifying its efforts to reinforce and bolster its troops, and to upgrade airstrips at Tanoua (Aouzou), Faya Largeau and Fada. The Libyans completed construction of an entirely new, major air base near water-place Wadi Doum. Once it was completed in early 1985, Wadi Doum AB and its 3,800 metre-long runway – consisting of sand hardened with crude oil, covered by aluminium grid, capable of supporting the heaviest aircraft in the LAAF arsenal (including Il-76 transports and Tu-22 bombers) – became the heart of Libyan deployment inside Chad. Protecting it were several early warning radar stations and a complete air defence brigade including one SA-6, one SA-8 and one SA-9 site, six ZU-23 23mm calibre flaks and a battery of ZPU-4 quarduple

A French reconnaissance photograph showing three Libyan BMP-1 IFVs and a T-55 MBT hidden in tree-shade in northern Chad. (Pierre-Alain Antoine Collection)

14.5mm anti-aircraft machine guns. At least four SF.260s and two Mil Mi-25 helicopter gunships were permanently deployed there, while LAAF fighter-bombers were rotated in and out on a temporary basis. For example, one Libyan Mirage F.1 squadron was deployed there between March and June 1985, and then replaced by an entire squadron of MiG-23s.[42]

Positioned in the very north of Chad, close to the internationally recognised border with Libya, Tanoua AB saw similar deployments. For example, in late 1984, it hosted a squadron each of Mirage F.1s and Su-22s. Although the LAAF decreased its presence at this air base for the next few months, it had another squadron of Su-22s and a detachment of at least two Tu-22s deployed there in early 1986.

Overall, Libyan troop strength in Chad in January 1986 was estimated at about 7,000 – including a number of often forcefully recruited expatriate workers grouped into the 'Islamic Legion' – supported by about 600 armoured vehicles. As well as in the Wadi Doum area, they were largely deployed around their bases in Fada and Faya Largeau.

For Oueddei's GUNT, 1985 was by no means a good one. While largely consisting of combatants from the Toubou tribe, this organisation was by no means a monolithic body. It included a sizeable group of former members of the insurgent Volcan Army, who were primarily Chadian Arabs led by Ahmed Acyl, and a large group of Christians from southern Chad, led by a former officer of official Army, Colonel Kamougue. Neither the Toubou nor the Christians ever felt comfortable with the Libyans: they considered the alliance with Tripoli as a temporary measure necessary to help them obtain control of N'Djamena and thus the country. Unsurprisingly, infighting between the three factions occurred time and again. In August and September 1985, a severe split appeared between Christians and others. When

Libyan attempts to mediate failed, Gaddafi ordered the LAAF into action. On 4 and 5 September 1985, Mirages and Sukhois repeatedly bombed Kamougue's positions in Faya Largeau. This effort misfired in a major way: nearly 5,000 Christian insurgents defected from the GUNT during the following months. Most of them surrendered to Habré's forces. Instead of insisting on their punishment, Habré integrated them into his armed forces. Some of the defectors were picked up by French Transall transports from northern Chad in secret nocturnal sorties in early 1986.[43]

What was left of the GUNT was a conventional military force consisting of about 2,000 truck-mounted light infantry, and a company of about 100 commandos. These were primarily deployed in the Tibesti, with a few small detachments immediately south of Fada and Faya Largeau. In order to cover-up the actual size of this small force, Libyans scrambled to create the image of an 'official army'. In early February 1986, Colonel el-Rifi, Director of Libyan Military Intelligence, toured a group of foreign journalists through northern Chad. Among others, these were shown about half a dozen SF.260s bearing the title 'GUNT Air Force', allegedly flown by 'Chadian GUNT pilots'.[44]

Of course, the aircraft and their crews were all Libyan and, overall, this action contributed little to lessening rivalries between different groups within the GUNT – primarily caused by increasing Libyan dominance.

Build-up of the FANT

The new Libyan offensive neither caught Habré unaware nor unprepared. On the contrary, during Opération Manta he launched a major effort to significantly expand and bolster the military capabilities of the FANT. The primary source for new arms was France, which shipped three large consignments of arms, ammunition, vehicles and various equipment in 1983, 1984 and 1985. Most of these were brought by ship to Cameroon and then air-lifted by Transall and Hercules transports to N'Djamena. Among weapons known to have reached the FANT in this period were about 78 vehicles and four AML-90 armoured cars that arrived in 1984.[45] Through 1985, the number of AML-90s was increased to about 15, with which the FANT became capable of establishing an official armoured squadron. However, at the same time Paris turned down Habré's request for Crotale SAMs. Instead, about 20 French-made Milan anti-tank guided missiles (ATGMs) and another squadron of refurbished AML-90s were furnished to N'Djamena through the French company ECAT in late 1985.[46]

Meanwhile, Habré continued collecting aid from many other parties. In 1984, he requested the provision of two C-130H Hercules transports from Washington to supplement the few available C-47s and Douglas C-54s. The Americans reacted by donating two refurbished C-130As, arguing these would be easier to maintain and better tailored to the limited maintenance capabilities available at N'Djamena. Chadians subsequently attempted to obtain additional C-130Hs, but in vain. Even so, the two C-130As proved of great value while providing support to subsequent FANT operations.[47]

Several shipments of light infantry weapons were also delivered from Iraq, usually on board transport aircraft of the Egyptian Air Force (EAF) directly to N'Djamena, together with a small team of Iraqi instructors. A small number of Chadian officers were also sent to Iraq for training.[48] Another party known to have provided arms and advice was Israel. The Israeli Defence Minister is said to have visited N'Djamena on 17 January 1983, arriving in the middle of the night on board an unmarked Boeing 707 of the IDF/AF from what was then Zaire (Democratic Republic of Congo since 1998). Another unmarked Boeing 707 is known to have landed at N'Djamena IAP on 21 April 1983, bringing a consignment of light weapons and a group of about a dozen of Israeli instructors who remained in Chad for three months. In May 1983, six Chadian officers were sent to Israel for training in intelligence operations. Since then, Mossad is said to have provided a continued, if limited flow of intelligence information to Chad.[49]

After negotiations with London for the provision of 15 second-hand Scorpion light tanks from Great Britain failed, the French

One of two C-130As donated to Chad by the USA in 1983. While taken at N'Djamena IAP (note the French Atlantic MPA in the background), immediately upon delivery, the Hercules is shown still wearing USAF insignia. (Albert Grandolini Collection)

Nearly all of the equipment provided to Habré's government by the USA and France in the mid-1980s was hauled to N'Djamena on USAF transports. Even the then biggest transport aircraft, like this Lockheed C-5A Galaxy, became a regular sight at N'Djamena IAP. (Albert Grandolini Collection)

decided to re-equip and reorganise the FANT in an entirely different fashion. Instead of armoured vehicles, they provided a large number of so-called 'technicals', mainly Toyota 4WDs. These were equipped with a wide range of heavy machine guns (such as 14.5mm calibre ZPU-1 and ZPU-4), light flak (for example 23mm calibre ZU-23) and large numbers of RPG-7s. In this fashion a highly mobile, spectacularly effective striking force came into being that was to dominate the battlefields of Chad through the second half of the 1980s. More than this, the spectacular tactics of the FANT were to prove highly influential for the future of warfare in much of the African continent.

Absent but Vigilant

While Habré's military situation in early 1986 was advantageous, that of France was far from ideal – at least in theory. In practice, Paris maintained sufficient military presence in the Central African Republic (CAR), Senegal and Djibouti to enable a quick reaction should the need arise.

Because of a host of negative experiences with Opération Manta, the government of President François Mitterrand was not particularly keen to become involved in Chad again. Manta proved a very cumbersome and costly enterprise, which was very unpopular with the French public. It included a large-scale airlift of about 3,000 ground troops, armoured vehicles and heavy equipment, air defence assets and supplies, supported by about 25 combat aircraft and an even larger number of helicopters. The strain of providing supplies for all these troops and equipment was immense: the French were forced to haul about 45,000 tonnes of cargo – nearly 80 percent of this consisting of fuel and water – to Chad each month, primarily with the help of Transall transports. Because of a complex set of ROEs and communication problems caused by immense distances, Manta stood in stark contrast to the most spectacular success of earlier French interventions in Chad – such as Opération Tacaud in 1981. It resulted in a situation that was the opposite of what was desired as France became involved in an inconclusive, open-ended major overseas military operation. The government in Paris and the French military authorities were keen never to permit this to happen again.

As their reconnaissance provided ever more evidence of Libyan activity related to Wadi Doum, the French began developing plans for an aerial strike on the air base. In February 1985, the staff of the Tactical Air Force (Force Aérienne Tactique, FATAC) of the French Air Force (Armée de l'Air, AdA) developed an initial plan, code-named Opération Pivert. It provided for eight SEPECAT Jaguar fighter-bombers equipped with BAP-100 anti-runway bombs, supported by several Boeing C-135F tankers and at least one Atlantic ELINT/SIGINT aircraft to fly an attack from airfields in Libreville (Gabon) and Bangui (CAR). Through September 1985, AdA Jaguars flew a series of related reconnaissance missions over northern Chad, code-named Musaraigne. Commandant André Carbon recalled a mission he flew in the company of Lieutenant Balandras on 8 September:

We flew very low, at only 180ft (54m), and descended to 160ft (48m) while over the target zone. Intelligence on types of threat in the target zone was rather vague and I vividly recall the tension going up by a notch while my wingman and [I] were underway within [the] Libyan air defence zone. Over Wadi Doum I was all the time looking behind him to make sure no missiles were tracking him. He did the same for me and I think we were not very proud of [ourselves] afterwards.[50]

Between 28 October and 11 November, the AdA gathered eight Jaguars necessary for Opération Pivert at Bangui IAP, but the attack was cancelled and the decision taken to increase the number of fighter-bombers to 12. Concerned about possible interference by LAAF interceptors deployed at Wadi Doum, the AdA flew additional reconnaissance sorties by Douglas DC-8 SARIGUE and Atlantic ELINT/SIGINT-gathering aircraft.[51] These detected

A Jaguar A (A142, coded 11-RO) of the EC 3/11 carrying a Harold reconnaissance pod under the centreline at the start of another reconnaissance mission over northern Chad in early 1986. (Photo by Robert Jeantrelle)

A pair of ZSU-23-4 'Shilka' self-propelled anti-aircraft guns of the Libyan Army on a parade in Tripoli in the early 1980s. (Tom Cooper Collection)

A row of vehicles from the SA-6 complex, including one carrying the 'Straight Flush' fire-control radar (foreground) and three carrying SAMs, on a parade in Tripoli in the early 1980s. When combined with Shilkas, they represented the highest threat to French aircraft flying low over northern Chad. (Tom Cooper Collection)

the presence of SA-6, SA-8 and SA-9 SAM-sites, ZSU-23-4 Shilka self-propelled anti-aircraft guns (SPAAGs) and five early warning radars – including one P-40 early warning radar (ASCC-code Long Track) with a range of 240km.

As soon as the additional Jaguars were in place, crews were put on alert again on 4 December. However, when their targeting intelligence was updated with the help of the latest information collected by ELINT/SIGINT aircraft which detected a P-18 early warning radar (ASCC-code Spoon Rest) active in the Faya Largeau area and a P-15 (ASCC-code Flat Face) operational in Fada – the attack on Wadi Doum was cancelled late on 5 December. Instead, the AdA launched two additional reconnaissance sorties on 7 December: one by Colonel Brun and Lieutenant Deltrieu, the other by Captains Antoine and Vinson. These missions, and another reconnaissance sortie flown on 11 December, discovered the presence of additional Libyan troops and vehicles along the planned route north of the 'Red Line'. Instead of attacking Wadi Doum, the French thus only flew a training mission – involving six Jaguars and four Mirage F.1C interceptors – against Awkaba airfield in the CAR on 19 December.[52]

Fourth Libyan Offensive in Chad

The new, combined Libyan-GUNT offensive into southern Chad was launched on 10 February 1986. As so often before, the insurgents were in the lead, with mechanised forces of the Islamic Legion and Libyan Army providing armour, logistic, communications and intelligence support from the rear. Supported by LAAF SF.260s and Mi-25s, the first insurgent attack resulted in the capture of Oum Chalouba, while the FANT garrison in Kouba Olanga came under severe pressure.

The GUNT attack came as no surprise for Habré: the Chadian president had requested assistance from Paris days earlier – and promptly received a positive reply.[53] The French not only put their forces in the CAR and Gabon on alert, but also troops from the 9th Marine Infantry and the 11th Parachute Division in France, and began converging these on Chad. The AdA did, however, take a few days to concentrate the necessary aircraft at Bangui IAP. While Commandant Carbon and Aspirant (Asp) Dardard conveyed two Jaguars from Libreville to Bangui on 12 February, six Jaguars scattered around Africa (including four deployed at Dakar IAP in Senegal) were flown to Bangui, together with a Boeing C-135F, on 14 February. It was in this fashion that the Barracuda Force came into being, consisting of 12 Jaguars from Escadre de Chasse (EC) 7 and EC.11, and four Mirage F.1C-200s from EC.1/5, all based at Bangui. Six C-135F tankers, one C-160 Transall NG, one Atlantic and a single Aérospatiale SA.330B Puma helicopter were readied at Libreville IAP in Gabon.

With such force in his back, Habré felt free to concentrate the FANT at Oued Fama and launch a major counter-attack on 13 February. The next day, his troops retook Oum Chalouba and forced the enemy to withdraw north of the 16th Parallel. With this, the fourth Libyan offensive into Chad collapsed after only four days.

Shocked by such a quick reversal of their allies, the Libyans hit

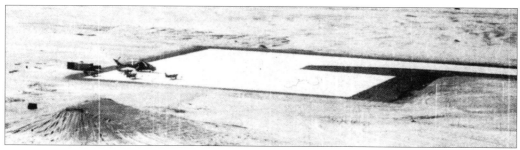

A French reconnaissance photograph showing a section of Wadi Doum AB where three SF.260 light strikers and a Mi-25 helicopter gunship are parked. In the foreground is one of the 'underground facilities': either a command centre or ammunition dump covered by sand. (Albert Grandolini Collection)

Another reconnaissance photograph showing a section of Wadi Doum AB with two parked Mi-25 helicopter gunships. (Andre Carbon Collection)

had to be kept at an absolute minimum. Ignoring local fuel and ammunition depots, and aircraft parked on the tarmac, they decided all the attack aircraft should concentrate solely on cratering the runway. Therefore eight of the Jaguars were each armed with 12 BAP.100 runway penetrating bombs, two RP.35 drop tanks with a capacity of 1,200 litre, a Phimat chaff and flare dispenser and a Barracuda jamming pod. Four others were loaded with two French-made SAMP-250 250kg calibre bombs, a single RP.35 drop tank under the centreline, Phimat and Barracuda pods. The purpose of deploying such weapons was to make big holes in the runway as a political signal to Tripoli. All 12 Jaguars also carried additional flare dispensers installed in their fins instead of braking parachutes, and Omera 40 reconnaissance cameras that were to take photographs to assess damage caused by the attack.

The plan for the strike on Wadi Doum was rather complex. The C-135Fs were to take off from Libreville and climb high above central Chad. While underway, they would be joined by Jaguars that launched from Bangui and refuel them twice while flying north. The strike had to be launched before 1000 local time because of the heavy load the Jaguars had to carry and the simmering heat in the CAR, which was decreasing their load-carrying capability. An additional important factor was that an early-morning strike would enable French pilots to attack their targets 'out of the sun' – disturbing the aim of Libyan gunners and delaying their reaction. French commanders expected that the Barracuda Force would lose two or three of its fighter-bombers.[54]

At 0530 on 16 February, the 12 Jaguars rolled for take-off from Bangui IAP. In the last moment before take-off, the aircraft piloted by Adjudant-Chef Saint Lanne suffered a malfunction of its auto-stabiliser, and the pilot was forced to abort the mission before even starting it. The other 11 continued and climbed to an altitude of 19,000ft (5,790m) before meeting three C-135Fs on their way north. After two refuellings and one re-calibration of their INS systems, the Jaguars descended to an altitude of only 200ft (60m) to avoid detection by P-18 radar at Wadi Doum, and accelerated to 450knots (833km/h).

About 30 miles (48km) from their target, the French fighter-bombers got into their attack formation – echelon to the left, with 10 seconds of separation between two flights – and, 10 miles (16.1km) away from Wadi Doum, accelerated to a speed of 500knots (926km/h). This compact formation appeared above the runway precisely at 0740 local time. There was absolutely no reaction from Libyan air defences; indeed, radar-warning-receivers (RWRs) of the Jaguars did not even detect any electronic emissions from Libyan radars.[55] All BAP-100s were dropped correctly, but several missed: while descending under parachutes, several were pulled away by hot air rising from the metalled runway, while a few

back in the usual fashion: at least four MiG-23s bombed FANT positions in Arada and Oum Chalouba on 15 February. With AdA Transalls and several chartered Boeing 707s about to start hauling additional arms and supplies to N'Djamena, the Libyan air strikes proved quite unpleasant for the French: there was certainly a chance of the LAAF sending its bombers to hit other places, further south inside Chad.

Keen to prevent the need for another operation like Manta, and interested in curbing the operations of Libyan interceptors and transport aircraft at Wadi Doum, but also in need of sending a decisive signal to Tripoli, the French concluded that Wadi Doum AB was again an interesting target. The raid on this air base was to be followed by a new intervention in Chad run under the code name Épervier (Sparrowhawk) – but this was to see a quick, sharp and decisive deployment of the military, with the key role being played by air power, while involvement of ground forces was kept to an absolute minimum.

Sparrowhawk against LAAF

In order to act quickly and forestall any further forward deployment of LAAF fighter-bombers, late on 15 February, Paris ordered the Barracuda Force to attack Wadi Doum AB at the earliest possible opportunity. AdA planners reacted by employing concentration of force and the element of surprise to achieve their objectives. Wadi Doum AB was to be rendered unusable for Libyan fighter-jets and transport aircraft for at least several days, while – for political reasons – the risk of captured or downed AdA pilots bombs malfunctioned and their parachutes never deployed. The leader of the second flight, Commandant André Carbon, recalled:

> Both flights dropping BAP-100s released right on target, but several bombs suffered from defective parachutes: this changed their trajectory and they missed the target. Nevertheless – and contrary to some rumours – the runway was rendered inoperational … During our attack, we saw a Mi-25 on the western end of the runway. This was attacked by my Number 4 – Lieutenant Hardouin – but his BAP-100s missed because of defective parachutes. That was quite frustrating.

Table 4: Composition of Barracuda-strike on Wadi Doum, 16 February 1986

Jaguar Serial Number	Code	Pilot	Position	Armament	Notes
Flight No. 1					
A84	11-YJ	Cdt de Tellier	leader	BAP-100	
A115	11-RH	Asp Lagenèbre	No. 2	BAP-100	
A112	11-RM	Capt Pellissier	No. 3	BAP-100	
A99	11-MQ	Lt Balandras	No. 4	BAP-100	
Flight No. 2					
A142	11-RO	Cdt Carbon	leader	BAP-100	
A92	11-RS	Asp Dardard	No. 2	BAP-100	
A108	11-MC	AdjCh Saint Lanne	No. 3	BAP-100	aborted before take-off
A140	11-EE	SLt Hardouin	No. 4	BAP-100	
Flight No. 3					
A87	11-RX	Capt Amourette	leader	SAMP-250	
A98	11-MT	Lt Schlitz	No. 2	SAMP-250	
A133	11-EF	Lt Debernardi	No. 3	SAMP-250	damaged
A91	11-YG	Capt Delcourt	No. 4	SAMP-250	damaged[57]

Only the last two Jaguar pilots made a mistake: they were late with their last turn before attack and thus appeared over the target with some delay. Both flew right into shrapnel and debris thrown up by SAMP-250 bombs dropped by the Leader and Number 2 of their formation, and suffered various degrees of damage. Lieutenant Schlitz realised that one of his SAMP-250s failed to drop during the attack and separated only while he was pulling away from the target. Nevertheless, all 11 Jaguars returned safely to Bangui after another in-flight refuelling operation over southern Chad, and a total flight time of 4¾ hours.[56]

Despite mishaps with BAP-100 bombs and damage suffered by

the last two Jaguars, the attack on Wadi Doum was a clear success. The runway was cratered in about a dozen places and out of service for nearly three weeks: it turned out that the replacement of aluminium plates was extremely cumbersome, requiring a disassembly of the entire runway to replace the damaged sections in its centre. Furthermore, one LAAF Mi-25 was damaged by nearby detonations of bombs. With Wadi Doum AB out of commission, the French were free to launch a major airlift and haul additional supplies for FANT to N'Djamena, along with their ground forces and other equipment.

The reasons for the success of Barracuda Force's attack on Wadi Doum were multiple. They included excellent training of officers and pilots, realistic planning based on very good intelligence and also years of preparation by the AdA for precisely such an event.The work on development of such ECM-pods as carried by Jaguars in Barracuda and Barax began in the late 1970s and resulted in France becoming one of the leading powers in this field. They were originally tested against some of the best

Jaguar A (A142/11-RO) from EC 3/11 'Corse' was the aircraft flown by Commander André Carbon during the attack on Wadi Doum on 16 February 1986. This rare photograph shows it in the similar configuration as during the mission: loaded with 18 BAP-100 runway-cratering bombs under the centreline. (Albert Grandolini Collection)

The A99/11-MQ from EC 2/11 'Vosges' was flown by Lieutenant Balandras, Number 4 in the first flight of Jaguars that attacked Wadi Doum AB. Like other aircraft in that formation, it was armed with BAP-100 runway-cratering bombs designed for deployment from low altitude. (Photo by Robert Jeantrelle)

The A92/11-RS from EC 3/11 'Corse' was flown by André Carbon's wingman, Aspirant Dardard, during the attack on Wadi Doum. (Photo by Robert Jeantrelle)

A dramatic photograph captured by Omera 40 camera of one of the Barracuda-Jaguars during the attack on Wadi Doum, showing two rows of BAP-100s hitting the runway of the Libyan airbase at an oblique angle – precisely as planned. (André Carbon Collection)

Detail from another photograph taken during the same attack, showing detonations of four BAP-100s on the runway, and three bombs still descending under their parachutes in the foreground. Parachutes were used to slow the BAP-100 so that the deploying aircraft could escape outside its lethal radius, but also to stabilise the bomb in a near-vertical position, before it was propelled by a small rocket motor through the runway surface and deep beneath it. In this fashion, the weapon detonates deep below the runway, creating a sizeable crater. (André Carbon Collection)

The small fleet of KC-135F tankers of the AdA provided support that was vital for the success of the strike on Wadi Doum AB. Notable on this photograph, taken at N'Djamena IAP later in 1986, is the original coat of silver-grey applied over the aircraft and its code 'CI' applied on the centre fuselage. (Photo by Robert Jeantrelle)

Detail photograph of the slightly unusual design of the in-flight-refuelling probe installed on Jaguar A. (Photo by Robert Jeantrelle)

Although designed and equipped as maritime patrol aircraft and ELINT/SIGINT-gatherers, good detection and tracking capabilities of their Iguane radars also made Atlantic aircraft of Aéronavale deployable as makeshift AEW platforms. This example is at N'Djamena IAP in 1986. (Photo by Robert Jeantrelle)

air defence systems the NATO had to offer, and in the course of joint Franco-German-US exercises at the testing grounds set up between Ramstein and Grostenquin. To further improve the effectiveness of these systems, France acquired several US-built threat generators that mimicked different Soviet-made radars within the frame of Project Peace Cognac in 1984. These included T-1A Mutes (Multiple Threat Emitter System) capable of simulating 60 different Soviet ground-based and aircraft-installed radars (the French ended up expanding their capacity to simulation of about 120 Soviet-made radars). The French also acquired several T-3 systems, capable of simulating Soviet-made FON-9 and SON-50 fire-control radars (ASCC-code Fire Can and Flap Wheel, respectively), and Gun Dish fire-control radars used to control anti-aircraft artillery.

Even radars of the newest Soviet design – like the 1S51M3-2 radar system of the SA-8 complex (ASCC-code Land Roll) were no big secret for the AdA because it took care to obtain the fourth – and last ever built – T-13 system, which was also capable of simulating Soviet-made SA-6s.

All French air force fighter pilots – but especially those flying Jaguars – were extensively trained in countering such weapons, along with US-made MIM-23B I-HAWKs, French Crotale and Italian-made Spada/Aspide SAM-systems. In the course of that training – which included French participation in one of the Red Flag exercises run in Nevada, USA, in 1981 they developed their own tactics of low-altitude, high speed attacks, considered paramount for their survival in a high threat environment. This comprised a formation manoeuvre known as 'double crankshaft',

developed by Commandant Pierre Amarger, which consisted of half the attack force breaking hard left while approaching the target, and then dropping chaff, and continuing steady for about 30 seconds before turning for actual attack in the target's direction. Simultaneously, the other half of the attack force would break right and mirror this manoeuvre. The French had realised that such manoeuvring was highly effective against SAM-systems like SA-6 and Crotale.

The double crankshaft was applied during attack on Wadi Doum AB. The only part of this scenario that did not work were the last two Jaguars that lagged behind, cut their turn in order to catch up with the rest of the formation and arrived at the time bombs dropped by formation members ahead of them began detonating.[58]

Revenge with Style

The loss of Wadi Doum AB could not have hit the LAAF at a worse point in time: instead of being able to utilise that runway to provide close air support for the GUNT, and bring in reinforcements and

A LAAF Tu-22 bomber like that which bombed the runway of N'Djamena IAP on 17 February 1986. (Albert Grandolini Collection)

A still from a video showing extensive damage caused by one of the Libyan bombs that hit the runway of N'Djamena IAP on 17 February 1986. (Albert Grandolini Collection)

supplies for the GUNT, their fighter jets and transports were limited to using Tanoua AB in northern Chad. Nevertheless, the LAAF hit back in most spectacular fashion.

Around 0700 on 17 February, a lone Tu-22 bomber thundered along the airliner corridor over Niger, then Nigeria, down the western border of Chad. Using international IFF mode, it approached undetected before descending to low altitude, accelerating to about 540knots (1,000km/h) and turning in the direction of N'Djamena IAP. The moment the bombardier opened the bomb bay to release his weapons, the newly-deployed AdA flak battery that was protecting the airport opened fire, apparently without coordination or any effect. The bomber released three FAB-1500 bombs (1,500kg/3.306lbs calibre). While two missed the airport and one of them failed to detonate, the third hit the runway, resulting in a crater some 8.5m deep and 25m in diameter.[59]

N'Djamena IAP was not closed by the strike, but this spectacular Libyan attack did cause some embarrassment for the French – and it took their engineers about 36 hours to repair the damage. Meanwhile, two Jaguars and two Mirage F.1Cs were deployed to the airport, where they landed safely, significantly bolstering its air defences.

The successful Tu-22 came away undisturbed and returned over northern Chad. Around that time, a US ELINT/SIGINT-reconnaissance aircraft flying over Sudan intercepted a distress call from the crew as they weres approaching Tanoua AB. Minutes later, a Libyan bomber crashed before reaching its destination. To this day, it remains unknown if this was the courageous Tu-22-crew that attacked N'Djamena, or the other one, which bombed

Kuba Olanga around the same time, which was lost in this fashion. It is also unknown if the bomber that flew the attack on the Chadian capital was hit by French flak, and nothing is known about the fate of the crashed Tupolev.[60]

Opération Tobus

On 18 February, AdA launched Opération Tobus, deploying a single Mirage IVA reconnaissance bomber of the Squadron for Reconnaissance and Instruction (Escadron de Reconnaissance et d'Instruction, ERI) to fly post-strike reconnaissance over Wadi Doum.[61] Because Libyan SA-6s at Wadi Doum could reach up to an altitude of 12,000m (39,370ft), the decision was taken for the aircraft, flown by Commandants Jacky Morel and Jules Mérouze on Mirage IVA serial number 31/BD, to make one high-altitude, supersonic pass over the target area.

The aircraft launched from France and was repeatedly refuelled in the air from a Boeing C-135F tanker while flying all the way over Egypt to Djibouti and then turning west. Over Africa, this small formation encountered bad weather, which caused the Boeing to veer off course. After some radio discussion between the two crews, trusting the better navigational system of the Boeing, the Mirage crew accepted a correction in their position of about 20 miles (32.2km), then Morel decided to separate from the tanker early. He took eight tonnes of fuel and accelerated over northern Ethiopia and Sudan in the direction of Chad. Above Sudan, he took a course 275, jettisoned empty fuel tanks and – while still 497 miles (800km) away from the target – began to accelerate to Mach 1.9 and climb to 15,240m (50,000ft).[62] Concerned about a possible navigational mistake and the lack of distinct terrain features that would aid in navigation with the help of his radar, the crew were happy to find that visibility was excellent and they could make minor adjustments in the course with the help of optical references. Approaching the target area, Morel and Mérouze realised they were exactly 20 miles too far south: luckily, they were still capable of correcting the route and passing directly above Wadi Doum.

About 5 hours and 15 minutes after take-off, the crew activated its high-altitude cameras (carried in a CT-52 container). The aircraft passed over the objective, turned around and began to decelerate. Shortly after, Morel noted a problem with fuel transfer and instruments showing a very low level in the manifolds. However, after checking all the circuit breakers several times, the gauges went up again and everything returned to normal. Back over Sudan, the Mirage met another C-135F tanker: after a high-speed dash over northern Chad, the reconnaissance bomber was left with less than 2,000 litres of fuel in its tanks. Morel and Mérouze then navigated their way back via Egypt, along the Libyan border and over the Mediterranean Sea, before an uneventful return to Bordeaux.

This was the longest reconnaissance mission ever carried out by a Mirage IVA: it lasted for 11 hours and covered 6,213 miles (10,000km), of which 30 minutes was at supersonic speed. The Mirage took no less than 48 tonnes of fuel from four C-135s in a total of 12 in-flight refuellings.

The Mirage IVA '31/BD', later in 1986, following re-application of national markings – removed during Opération Tobus. Notable is the unusual, oblique-facing radome for attack/navigation radar installed underneath the fuselage between the intakes and the aft cockpit. (US Navy photo)

Libyan MiG-25RB-pilot with his aircraft. In February 1986, the LAAF was still bold enough to send its 'Foxbats' over N'Djamena IAP. This was to change during the following months – because of increased pressure by the USN in the Mediterranean and the presence of French MIM-23B I-HAWK SAMs in Chad. (Albert Grandolini Collection)

The Libyans were faster in reacting this time: later the same day, a single LAAF MiG-25R thundered high above N'Djamena, right at the moment the French were unloading their Crotale SAMs at the local airport, while several Jaguars and Mirage F.1s were in the process of landing. The Jaguars in question were led by Commandant André Carbon:

On 18 February 1986, I made a flight from Bangui to N'Djamena, with Aspirant Dardard as wingman. The same afternoon we made an armed reconnaissance sortie north-west of N'Djamena.

It seems that a day later, the LAAF attempted to re-attack this airport, again with Tu-22s, but that the mission failed early on. While the Libyans claim that the Tu-22 was detected while approaching N'Djamena and forced to withdraw when AdA scrambled two Mirages, French officers deployed in Chad do not recall any kind of Libyan contacts on this day.

Nevertheless, the successful LAAF strike of 17 February was enough to convince French commanders that the crucially important airport was in need of better protection. Therefore, a

MIM-23B I-HAWK battery of the 403 Artillery Regiment of the French Army (403e Régiment d'Artillerie) was deployed from Chaumont to N'Djamena IAP in Lockheed C-5A Galaxy transports of the US Air Force between 28 February and 3 March. By this time, the AdA already had 10 Jaguars, six Mirage F.1Cs, one Atlantic and seven C.160 Transalls there. A further six Jaguars, six C.160s and one Atlantic were based at Bangui, while two C-135Fs and two C.160s were deployed to Libreville.

On the ground, French deployment during this early phase of Opération Épervier was much more limited. The initial contingent included only about 600 troops, primarily members of the 2nd Airborne Regiment of Foreign Legion (2e REP, Régiment Etranger Parachutiste), a squadron of armoured cars, artillery and logistic units. The rest of the combat troops came from the 9e DIMa that secured N'Djamena IAP, and a Syracuse mobile communications station with security force in the form of a company of airborne troops from the 11th Parachute Division (Division Parachutiste, DP). As in the case of the deployment of French-operated MIM-23B I-HAWK SAMs, C-5As and Lockheed C-141 StarLifters of the USAF contributed significantly to the deployment of French ground forces to Chad.[63]

When insurgents launched their last attack on Oum Chalouba, this was easily repelled by the FANT on 5 March 1986. An attack by Habré's forces on the forward GUNT base in Chicha ended in a swift victory over three battalions of the Islamic Legion and heavy material losses for Libyan forces on 17 March. By this time, Mirage F.1CR reconnaissance fighters of the EC.33, AdA, were also at N'Djamena IAP. They flew their first operational sortie over the Fada area a week later.

The overall cost of Opération Épervier was low, with minimal material losses. The French air force is known to have lost only one aircraft: a Jaguar, serial number A152/11-RG, crashed on 27 March during take-off from Bangui after losing thrust. While its pilot, Lieutenant Michael Etcheberry, ejected safely, sadly, the aircraft crashed into apartment buildings nearby, killing 22 civilians.

Opération Épervier thus proved highly effective – to a large degree due to the success of the French strike on Wadi Doum AB. Deploying only minimum military force, the French not only stabilised the situation by deterring the Libyans from involving larger contingents of their military, but also prevented the LAAF from supporting the GUNT. The Libyans found themselves in no position to respond in fashion – and only days later were themselves exposed to a new threat from the US Navy in the Mediterranean too.

R440 Crotale

The combat complement of each Crotale SAM-site consisted of up to three 12-tonne, armoured combined launch and command guidance vehicles (TELARs) made by Hotchkiss, and an acquisition vehicle carrying the Thomson-CSF Mirador IV coherent pulse-Doppler surveillance and target designation radar (operating in S-band). All vehicles were electrically powered 4x4s, with each wheel having its own thermal motor driving an alternator. This method of propulsion resulted in lower vibration levels and more flexible driving; it also permitted sealing of the vehicle for full NBC-protection. A hydraulic circuit provided power-assisted steering, braking, vehicle suspension and automatic levelling by jacks. Each vehicle was fully air-conditioned.

The heart of the site is the vehicle carrying the Mirador IV radar. This has a range of 18.5km for targets flying at levels between zero and 3,000m. Its antenna rotates at a speed of 60 rotations per minute. When it became operational, it was a very light yet sophisticated system with subclutter visibility of only 60dB, a separation capability on a bearing of 3.5 and accuracy of information of +/- 0.3 degrees in bearing and +/- 3 degrees in position. Data processing was run by an SN-1050 computer and the system had no less than 12 tracking channels. A crew of only two or three was required to man this vehicle, including a chief operator, assistant operator (if required) and driver.

Associated with Mirador IV was an automatic target evaluation system that provided the system with a very fast reaction time. The radar was also equipped with an IFF-interrogator (and decoder), a non-saturable extractor and a real-time digital computer (identical with that used in the TELAR) used for generation of synthetic video symbols and for the continuous processing of the system's track-while-scan loops (used for the generation of accurate target data and for confirmation of threat evaluation).

Up to three TELARs could be served by a single acquisition vehicle. Data-transmission to the firing units was provided by digital link – either by cable (out to 400m) or by radio (from 50 to 5,000m). The entire SAM-site required around six minutes to become operational from the moment it stopped moving.

Each TELAR carried four ready-to-fire missiles stored inside containers that served as launchers. Installed concentrically with the launcher turret of each TELAR was a monopulse fire-control Ku-band ecartometric radar with range of 16km for targets with a radar-cross section of 1m². This radar was capable of guiding two missiles simultaneously towards the same target – which in turn meant that each Crotale SAM-site could simultaneously engage four different targets with up to eight missiles.

Table 5: Equipment of a typical R.440 Crotale SAM-site, 1986

Equipment and remarks	Number of items per site (battalion)
fire control vehicle	1
TELAR	3
X-band tele-command transmitter	1
IR-gathering system	1
TV-tracking system	1
real-time digital computer	1
operating console	1

The purpose of the Crotale TV-tracking system was to support operations if for some reason – such as electronic countermeasures – radar tracking was impossible. The digital computer was used to align the radar on target, make parallax corrections to the target designation data and generate guidance orders for the missile and its fuse. The operating console consisted of a PPI display for the air situation – providing the operator with a threat indicator (level of threat, initiated targets and IFF-response) and a video map showing locations of the firing units – and an operation panel with lamps indicating the status of firing units, 'fire' push-buttons and self-destruction push buttons (so the operator could order self-destruction of the missile in flight in case of late IFF-recognition).

The weapon for the Crotale SAM-site was the R.440 missile. This was a single-stage, solid propellant vehicle guided by command guidance via a digital radio link. It was packed in ready-to-use condition into a container that weighted 100kg. The missile was 2.98m long, with wing span of 0.54m and launch weight of 85kg. It carried a warhead of 15kg over a maximum range of 12km.

The fire-control vehicle of a French Crotale SAM-site in position in Chad. (via Albert Grandolini)

A TELAR of a French Crotale SAM-site in combat position, atop an earthen mound. (via Albert Grandolini)

CHAPTER 5
PRAIRIE FIRE

In mid-March 1986, US Navy units in the Mediterranean began preparations for Operation Attain Document III. As usual, this was announced to the Libyan authorities in advance. Scheduled to last from 23 to 29 March, it was intended to become a large-scale FON exercise, involving three carrier battle groups and a surface action group (SAG), with aircraft and ships operating south of the 'Line of Death', thus discrediting Libyan claims over the Gulf of Syrte while demonstrating US resolve in the struggle against international terrorism. While the White House and the Pentagon saw Attain Document III as an excellent opportunity to provoke a military confrontation with Libya, the commander of the US 6th Fleet, Vice Admiral Frank B. Kelso, became extremely concerned about a possible all-out attack on TF-60. He requested an adaptation of ROEs to a level where he would be given the authority to conduct pre-emptive operations against any threat that become apparent, even if the Libyans did not open fire first. This request was endorsed by nearly all of Kelso's senior commanders and authorised by President Reagan, who also approved a contingency operation code-named Prairie Fire, comprising graduated responses to various levels of Libyan actions. Emboldened by such permission, Kelso developed a plan according to which not only were ships to operate south of the 'Line of Death', but aircraft of the USN were to fly right up to the international 12-mile limit off the Libyan coast.[64]

On 19 March, the carrier battle group centred around aircraft carrier USS *America* (CV-66), commanded by Rear Admiral Henry H. Mauz Jr, joined USS *Coral Sea* and USS *Saratoga* in the central Mediterranean to create Task Force Zulu. As well as carriers, positioned in an eastwest line approximately 150 miles (240km) north of the 'Line of Death', this task

USS *America* (CV-66, background), in the company of guided missile destroyer USS *Preble* (DDG-46), in early 1986. (US Navy photo)

An E-2C Hawkeye of VAW-123 'Screwtops' preparing for catapult start from USS *America* in March 1986. (US Navy photo)

USS *Yorktown* (CG-48), one of two Ticonderoga-class guided missile cruisers that took part in Operation Attain Document III, in March 1986. Their SPY-1 three-dimensional radars greatly enhanced the radar coverage around the USN's CVBGs. (US Navy photo)

force included the flagship of the 6th Fleet, USS *Coronado* (AGF-11), four guided missile cruisers, three guided missile destroyers, one destroyer, three guided missile frigates and nine other frigates, with a total of 27,000 officers, sailors and Marines on board. Each carrier was scheduled to run flight operations for about 16 hours a day, with *America* covering the period from 1200 until 0345, *Saratoga* from 2015 until 1200 and *Coral Sea* from 0345 until 2015. Together, the three carrier air wings on board were to continuously keep 12 CAP aircraft, eight SUCAP aircraft, four Lockheed S-3A Viking anti-submarine warfare aircraft, two E-2Cs, two EA-6Bs and two Sikorsky SH-3H Sea King anti-submarine warfare helicopters airborne around the clock. Furthermore, the USN intended to keep up to 14 CAP stations – all within the Tripoli FIR – occupied by day, of which two were inside the northern portion of the Gulf of Syrte, while a dedicated E-2C was to coordinate surface operations.[65]

After the earlier tensions, and especially the encounters between USN aviators and LAAF interceptors during Operation Attain Document II, there was plenty of anticipation in squadron-ready rooms of all three aircraft carriers. David 'Hey Joe' Parsons recalled:

> The MiGs and other Libyan fighters had been very active against *Saratoga*'s F-14s (VF-74 and VF-103) so we were certain that we'd see more of [the] same when we arrived on *America* in March. We were so sure that I designed a kill marking scheme (green circle and black plan view of respective aircraft) and fashioned cardboard silhouettes of all the type fighters in service with [the] Libyans.

Further south was the SAG comprising the brand-new Aegis-class guided missile cruiser USS *Ticonderoga* (CG-47), guided missile destroyer USS *Scott* (DDG-995) and destroyer USS *Caron* (DD-970). Like USS *Yorktown* (CG-48) that was at sea with the carriers, *Ticonderoga* was one of the most modern warships in the world, equipped with highly sophisticated AN/SPY-1 multipurpose phased array radar, which vastly enhanced radar coverage to a range of 200 miles (321km). These three ships were planned to cross the 'Line of Death'.

Table 6: Composition of CVW-1 (USS *America*), 10 March 1986 – 10 September 1986

Aircraft Carrier	Carrier Air Wing & Squadrons	Aircraft Type & Modex	Duration of Deployment & Notes
USS *America* (CV-66)	**CVW-1**	(AB)	10 March 1986 – 10 September 1986
	VF-102 Diamondbacks	F-14A AB100	
	VF-33 Starfighters	F-14A AB200	
	VA-47 Clansmen	A-7E AB300	
	VA-72 Blue Hawks	A-7E AB400	
	VA-34 Blue Blasters	A-6E & KA-6D AB500	
	VAW-123 Screwtops	E-2C AB600	
	VMAQ-2 Playboys	EA-6B AB600	
	HS-11 Dragonslayers	SH-3H	
	VQ-2 Batmen Det. ?	EA-3B JQ10	embarked March–April 1986

Libyan Air Defence Command

Libya began the work of establishing an integrated air defence system (IADS) in 1977, with the intention to cover most of the Mediterranean coast between Tripoli and Tobruk, but also all major bases in the centre and south of the country. For this purpose, immense numbers of radars, surface-to-air missiles, communication and other related equipment were imported, with the intention of creating an Air Defence Force as a separate branch of the Libyan armed forces. The first shipments of Soviet-made SAMs arrived in Libya in early 1977, together with a sizeable team of instructors under the command of Lieutenant-Colonel Vladimir Markov.[66]

Soviet reports indicate that Libya purchased enough equipment for no less than 86 battalions equipped with 276 launchers for S-76MK (ASCC-code SA-2 Guideline) and S-125M1A (ASCC-code SA-3 Goa) SAMs. These systems were reinforced through the addition of an unknown number of French-made Crotale SAMs and Soviet-made 2K12 Kub (ASCC-code SA-6 Gainful) and 9K33 Romb (ASCC-code SA-8 Gecko) systems, all of which were mobile. Not only air defence units, but all units of the Libyan Arab Army were further protected by 23mm calibre ZSU-23-4 Shilka self-propelled, radar-controlled anti-aircraft quad-guns and large numbers of teams equipped with 9K32 Strela-2 (ASCC-code SA-7 Grail) MANPADS.[67]

Although at least a quarter of about 2,000 Soviet advisers present in Libya in 1985 were busy supporting the emerging service, the build-up of the Libyan IADS was still incomplete, primarily due to the lack of qualified personnel. Nevertheless, two local air defence systems – 'air defence divisions' in Soviet military vocabulary – were operational, one covering Tripoli and the other Benghazi. The division protecting Tripoli is known to have comprised seven battalions equipped with 42 launchers for S-75MKs, 12 battalions with 48 launchers for S-125M1As, three battalions with 16 TELs (48 launchers) for Kubs, one regiment equipped with OSA-AK and two battalions with 60 SA-7. These were supported by an appropriate number of early-warning radars, including P-12, P-14F, P-15, P-18, P-19, P-35, P-37 and P-40, and height-finding radars including PRV-11, PRV-13 and PRV-16, all of which were integrated with the help of an information collecting and display system provided by German company Telefunken, supported by an elaborate system of wireless and cable communications.[68]

All these systems provided near unlimited radar coverage out to about 350km around Tripoli and Benghazi down to altitudes between 300 and 500m above the Mediterranean. At ranges out to about 50km, radars deployed around Tripoli and Benghazi were capable of detecting targets down to an altitude between 50 and 100m.

To further enlarge the envelope of these two divisions, the Soviets

A Hungarian military delegation visiting a Libyan SA-3 site outside Misurata in the mid-1980s. (Robert Szombati Collection)

Libyan SA-6 missiles in Tripoli during a military parade in the mid-1980s. (Albert Grandolini Collection)

delivered equipment for four battalions of V-200VE Vega long-range SAMs in 1985.[69] One of these became operational by early 1986 and was positioned near the Ghurdabiyah AB, outside Syrte, in combination with at least two SA-2 and several other SAM-sites.

All major air bases in southern Libya, and all Libyan ground units deployed in Chad, were as well-protected, usually by a combined air defence brigade including a battalion each of SA-6 and SA-8s, supported by ZSU-23-4s and SA-7s, and associated early warning radars.

S-200VE Vega-E/SA-5b Gammon

The S-200VE Vega-E was an export variant of the S-200 Angara long-range surface-to-air system, code-named SA-5 Gammon by the ASCC. It was a medium to long-range SAM belonging to the second generation of Soviet SAMs, developed to complement the SA-2 system. The Soviets began exporting the S-200VE to Syria and Libya only when a much more advanced replacement became available in the form of the S-300 (ASCC-code SA-10) system.

As deployed in Libya, a standard SA-5b battalion (one SAM-site) was integrated within a brigade equipped with SA-2s and SA-3s, yet connected directly to the brigade's command post and the entire air defence system via the Seznes-50 automatic fire-control system. Alternatively, every SA-5b site was able to operate on its own.

7: Equipment of a typical Libyan S-200VE Vega-E SAM site, 1986

Equipment and remarks	Number of items per site (battalion)
K9B command post	1
K1B acquisition system coupled w P-37 early warning radar	1
K2B fire-control command post	1
P-37 early warning radar	1
P-14 early warning and acquisition radar	1
PRV-17 height-finding radar	1
K1B ('Square Pair') fire-control radar	2
5P72B launcher	6

Other equipment of a typical SA-5 site included K3B containers with missile and launcher-control equipment, and 5N24M

missile-carrying trucks required to haul reload rounds. Each site had only two reloads (a total of 12 missiles), though these could be brought into action within only two minutes with the help of a semi-automatic reloading system.

Typical engagement procedure began with P-37 detecting the target and establishing its precise position with the help of the PRV-17 height-finder. Data from P-37 and PRV-17 was then downloaded to the K9 command post (the nerve centre of each SA-5 site) and then forwarded to the K2 fire-control command post, which controlled two K1 Square Pair fire-control radars (some of the highest-powered fire-control radars in the world, with peak power output of up to 2Megawatt). Each of the Square Pairs worked on a different channel, meaning that each site could simultaneously engage two different targets with up to three missiles.

Guidance of the V-880E missile was provided by radio command during the initial flight phase; the missile then received mid-course correction signals from Square Pair radar, followed by semi-active radar homing in the terminal phase of the flight.

The V-880E was a massive single-stage vehicle with a length of 10.72m, wing-span of 2.85m and body diameter of 0.85m, weighing 7,100kg on launch. Four solid-fuelled strap-on rocket boosters, each 4.9m long and 0.48m in diameter, fell off after propelling the missile to a speed of about Mach 4: the range of boosters determined the minimal engagement range of the entire system, which was about 17km. After separation of boosters, a dual-thrust solid-fuelled rocket motor was ignited, which brought the missile to its maximum range of about 240km. Weighing 217kg, the HE warhead was detonated either by command signal or the onboard proximity fusing system.

A still from a video showing four 5N24M missile-carrying trucks loaded with V-880E missiles during a parade in Tripoli in the mid-1980s. (Albert Grandolini Collection)

F-14 vs MiG-25

Operation Attain Document III commenced at 0100 local time on 23 March. During the day, all USN aircraft remained north of 32° 30'. To the surprise of almost everybody on board USN warships, there was no Libyan reaction, as explained by Parsons:

> The Libyans got quite shy after we got three carriers on line in the Gulf of Syrte. But, our CO was VERY aggressive and we pressed the ROE to the limit. He even had the Libyan control tower frequency in one of his radios and taunted the Libyans at Benghazi to come out and play.

What happened was that as soon as the Pentagon announced Operation Attain Document III, the LAAF dispersed most of its Mirages, MiG-21s and MiG-23s to air bases in the centre of the country.[70] For example, only one out of three MiG-23 squadrons usually based at Benina AB outside Benghazi was left at that base: the other two were evacuated to southern Libya. The exact reasons for this decision remain unknown, but it seems that Gaddafi and his military commanders expected US attacks on Libyan air bases. Their decision was quite ironic considering the LAAF had no less than eleven fully-developed air bases along the Mediterranean coast, and was thus well-dispersed even in peacetime.

When no LAAF interceptors were scrambled, around 2015 Tomcats from the *Saratoga* and the *America* crossed the 'Line of Death' several times, occupying two CAP stations over the Gulf of Syrte, one of them about 60 miles (96.5km) off the Libyan coast. Once again, there was no Libyan reaction. It was only hours later that the Libyan SA-5 SAM-site near Syrte powered up its Square Pair early warning radar and locked-on USN aircraft. All radar and electronic warfare officers in Task Force Zulu watched their scope in anticipation of the Libyans opening fire. However, contrary to expectations, the Libyans did not move.

With the situation remaining calm, Kelso ordered the SAG into action. At noon on 24 March, *Ticonderoga*, *Scott* and *Caron* crossed the 'Line of Death under protection of Tomcats that flew CAPs, and Corsairs and Intruders that flew SUCAPs. Among the F-14s that crossed the 'Line of Death' in support of the SAG was the Tomcat flown by Deputy Commander VF-33, Lieutenant Commander Michael 'Smiles' Bucchi, with RIO Lieutenant Commander Ken 'Heimy' Heimgartner. Another pilot from their unit recalled about their mission:

> Smiles and Heimy were already legends between Tomcat crews. During that sortie, they flew an aircraft equipped with the TCS. That is a stabilised video camera with telescopic lens installed under the nose of the Tomcat, which enabled them to visually identify such aircraft as MiG-25 in clear weather from several dozen kilometres away. The TCS was brand new and very expensive, and our squadron had only three aircraft equipped with one (we got many more of these sets when *Saratoga* out-chopped [left the Mediterranean]). That was the way it was even back then: not enough gear to go around – and this was during the 'go-go- buildup' of the Reagan years.

Smiles and Heimy flew the F-14A serial number 161142, modex AB200, which was the best aircraft in [the] squadron and equipped with TCS. Their wingman flew the Tomcat serial number 159021, modex AB206: that was an elderly jet that spent much of that cruise in the hangar together with another 'senior, 159010/AB207. It had no TCS.

Contrary to usual practice within the US Air Force, where the war-load of all involved aircraft is de-facto dictated from above, top USN commanders left their squadrons to decide about their armament. Parsons explained:

> Among the F-14 crews aboard the *America*, there were some differences in terms of the weapons load. In VF-102, we preferred to arm our Tomcats with Sparrows and Sidewinders only. We were expecting to fly escorts and engage in dogfights and wanted to have our machines as light as possible. The VF-33 preferred the 2/2/2 configuration instead: two Sidewinders, two Sparrows and two long-range Phoenix missiles. They wanted to be ready to use [the] much vaunted Phoenix if there was a chance, even if this increased the weight of their aircraft.

The two Tomcats led by Bucchi barely reached the intended CAP station when their crews nearly got an opportunity to put Phoenix missiles to the test. When the USN's SAG violated what Libyans considered their territorial waters, two MiG-25PDS forward-deployed at Benina AB were scrambled with the order to shoot down all airborne intruders, as recalled by Ali Thani:

> I did not expect us to be successful but was determined to carry out my orders. We climbed to 6,000m (19,685ft). The GCI vectored us to about 30km from the nearest target and then ordered me to activate my radar, acquire a target and open fire. This was my first encounter with Tomcats and I was expecting them to be armed with Phoenix missiles. For this reason, I decided not to lock-on on them and fire one of my R-40RDs, but instead wanted to get closer and wait for an opportunity to deploy my short-range R-60MKs ... While approaching, we manoeuvred as so often before: whenever they turned to one side, the GCI redirected us. This was repeated several times until we got closer and I turned directly towards one of [the] Tomcats, trying to lock-on with a missile. It did not work, because the Tomcat disappeared from my view too soon.

Although MiG-25s are not particularly manoeuvrable aircraft, their aggressive manoeuvring during approach, 'painting' of USN aircraft with their radars and facing F-14s head-on was a clear show of hostile intention. However, because Admiral Kelso has not yet issued the necessary code-word, his new ROEs were not yet in force – which meant that MiGs had to open fire first for Tomcats to fire at them. This left Bucchi and his wingman with no alternative but to outmanoeuvre their opponents. Turning around, the two Tomcats dragged the MiGs into a descent to about 5,000ft (1,524m), where they enjoyed a huge advantage

An F-14A Tomcat from VF-33 in full afterburner, just milliseconds away from being launched from catapult No. 3 of USS *America*, off Libya, in March 1986. Notable is the armament consisting of an AIM-7 Sparrow (underneath the right wing) and an AIM-54A Phoenix missile. (US Navy photo)

Another Tomcat from VF-33 (one of the few that was equipped with the TCS camera system, installed inside a housing underneath the radome), shortly before launching from USS *America*, armed with AIM-7F and AIM-9L missiles, during Operation Attain Document III. (US Navy photo)

A missed opportunity: two stills from the TCS-video of a Libyan MiG-25PDS intercepted by Bucchi and Heimgartner on the early afternoon of 24 March 1986. At the time, the TCS-recorder had a pretty limited recording time (about 3 minutes), but the video it produced was obviously spectacular. (US Navy release)

in manoeuvrability, and then took position at their opponents' 'six o'clock' – directly behind two Libyans. While Bucchi was manoeuvring to keep his opponent in sight, and switching his weapons selector to 'guns', Heimgartner reported 'excessive hostile actions and intent' to the E-2C, and requested permission to open fire. His report was forwarded to the *America*. The lead MiG-25 – the one flown by Thani – meanwhile turned slowly to the right, followed by his wingman, before reversing to the left. While Bucchi followed, Heimgartner again asked for permission to fire. Minutes passed without reply, as the lead Tomcat continued manoeuvring behind the lead MiG-25. Then both MiGs switched on their afterburners, made a sharp turn to the left and disappeared in a southern direction. By the time the air-warfare commander from the *America* granted permission for the Tomcats to open fire and added, 'take the bastards on', the two F-14As were already on their way back to tanker aircraft.

SA-5 Attack

As the two MiG-25s were withdrawing, a pair of F-14As from VF-102 reached the same CAP-station previously held by the pair from VF-33, about 68.3 miles (110km) from the Libyan coast. This time there was a near-instantaneous reaction from the Libyan SA-5 site positioned near Syrte. David Parsons recalled what happened around 1352 local time:

We were underway on the wing of Roy 'Flash' Gordon who flew with skipper, Mike 'Sparky' Lyle, as RIO. Once on station, we flew a race-track pattern. Flash and Sparky were flying south, we north, when Sparky's AWG-9 radar picked up a contact about 100km (62.1

miles) away. Flash turned in, thinking this would be another MiG-25 coming directly at him. Sparky locked-on the target and Flash followed the target-symbol in head-up display (HUD) to see the target accelerating through Mach 1, then Mach 2, Mach 3 ... then he spotted a vertical contrail. [A] moment later, we received a coded message via data-link, that the Libyans have fired a SA-5 at us. That's when we realised the radar contact must be an SA-5. We retired northwards via Split-S manoeuvre while other assets confirmed our 'diagnosis'.

Much later, Soviet sources reported that three USN aircraft entered Libyan airspace and that Gaddafi personally issued the order for the SA-5 battalion positioned outside Syrte to open fire. Two missiles were fired against targets that were 105km away: because the targets disappeared from the display and the Libyans – and their Soviet advisors – subsequently reported activity of USN 'rescue helicopters', Tripoli concluded that 'target was destroyed'.[71]

Actually, no USN aircraft was hit, but with this action the Libyans committed a deliberately hostile act, opening an opportunity for the Americans to hit back in force. Kelso did

A row of F-14s from VF-33 (including AB211 and AB207) and VF-102 (AB106 and AB105), together with a KA-6D from VA-34 (background), on the afterdeck of USS *America* during Operation Attain Document III. (US Navy photo)

KA-6D Intruder tankers from all three aircraft carriers remained busy supporting other USN aircraft throughout Operation Attain Document III. This example was one of three KA-6Ds assigned to VA-55, embarked on USS *Coral Sea*. (US Navy photo)

flanked by Libyans from the east and west. After opening fire, the Libyans were also likely to expect an immediate retaliation and thus be primed for action. Midway through preparations for the counter-attack, Kelso received a message from the C-in-C LAAF, Colonel Salleh Abdullah Salleh, forwarded via commercial telex:

Unless the aggressive acts are stopped against Jamahiriyya we are bound to destroy the CV carriers / Stop / In doing that will have the political and military support of the world states / Stop / Maintain peace and you will leave in peace / Stop / Best regards [73]

not react immediately: only after receiving confirmation that the Libyan SA-5 site indeed locked-on to the Tomcats, and that the firing was therefore no accident, did he send a flash precedence message to Task Force Zulu, executing 'table top', around 1538. In this fashion he authorised the fleet to 'engage Libyan units closing the force in international waters and airspace'.[72] The game was now on, and the following action was to spread like a 'prairie fire'.

Night of the Boats

Although in possession of authority to attack the SA-5 site near Syrte, the commander of the 6th Fleet USN decided to wait for the night. The SAM site was positioned near the southern coast of the Gulf of Syrte, which meant that any US aircraft approaching it could be

Shortly after receiving this threat, Kelso ordered Jeremiah to destroy the SA-5 site near Syrte. Around 1830, two A-7Es armed with AGM-88 HARMs were launched for attack. Fifteen minutes later, the Libyans fired one SA-5 at a pair of USN Corsairs that were approaching the coast. Realising the moment of surprise was lost, Jeremiah immediately cancelled this attack and ordered both fighter-bombers to return to their carrier. The Libyans kept on firing, nevertheless: one SA-2 was launched around 1855 and a fourth SA-5 around 1914. Both missiles were jammed by a

Because of very intensive LAAF operations during Attain Document II, when the USN returned to the Gulf of Syrte in March 1986, its units began arming their aircraft 'for all eventualities'. So it happened that even A-6E Intruders – like this example from VA-55, seen shortly before landing aboard USS *Coral Sea* – began carrying AIM-9L Sidewinder air-to-air missiles (left outboard pylon), in addition to the more usual AGM-84 Harpoon anti-ship missiles (left inboard pylon) and Mk.20 Rockeye CBUs. (US Navy photo)

combination of effective ECM and evasion manoeuvring of USN fighters.

Kelso, Jeremiah and subordinate officers were still in the process of preparing the next attack on the SA-5 site when an E-2C and USS *Ticonderoga* almost simultaneously reported establishing contact with *Waheed* (hull number 526), a French-built Combattante IIG-class fast attack craft/missile (FACM) of the Libyan Navy exiting the port of Misurata at a speed of 24 knots (44.4km/h). Carrying four Italian-made Otomat Teseus Mk. 1 or Mk. 2 turbojet-powered anti-ship missiles with a practical range of 37 miles (60km), and a warhead of 210kg (460lb), *Waheed* packed a powerful punch and was almost within striking range of the USN's SAG.[74] The E-2C therefore vectored two SUCAP sections – one consisting of two A-6Es from VA-34, armed with AGM-84A Harpoon anti-ship missiles, the other of two A-6Es from VA-85, carrying Mk.20 Rockeye CBUs – to intercept. After finding *Waheed* on his radar, the pilot of one of the Harpoon-armed A-6Es called the *Saratoga* to verify permission to fire. The carrier responded instantly, 'The admiral says, "Smoke 'em"'.

At 2017, the lead Intruder fired a single AGM-84A from a range of 16 miles (25.7km). Skimming the surface at a speed of 650mph (1,050kmph, the missile approached *Waheed* undetected, then jinked upwards before diving for attack: it thumped into the superstructure of the 260-tonne vessel, exploding a fraction of a second later, well inside the hull. Already wrecked by the

Harpoon-hit, *Waheed* was then devastated by Rockeyes released by two A-6Es from VA-85, around 2030. The next day, 17 survivors were rescued by Spanish tanker *SS Castillo de Ricote*.

Parsons recalled what happened next:

Then we began making high-speed runs at [the] Libyans to get a reaction from the SA-5 site.

Around 2100, four A-7Es from the *Saratoga* approached the Libyan coast: two from VA-81, lead by Commander, CVW-17, Brodsky, flew high and in full view of Libyan radars. Brodsky recalled:

It was a beautiful night. I was about 50 miles away from the SA-5, and I was sure I could have seen a launch. [75]

The Libyans took the bait and their Square Pair radars locked-on on two high-flying Corsairs. However, with this they only exposed themselves to attack by two low-flying A-7Es from VA-83, led by the CO of that unit, Commander Richard J. Nibe. From a range of 37 miles (59.5km), each Corsair fired one AGM-88A that homed on the radar beam of the Square Pairs at twice the speed of sound. While one HARM narrowly missed, the other scored a direct hit on the radar antenna, demolishing it completely. The SA-5 site immediately went offline. Parsons commented:

A group of 'red shirts' – weapon handlers – loading an AGM-84A Harpoon anti-ship missile on one of the A-6E from VA-55 on USS *Coral Sea* in March 1986. (US Navy photo)

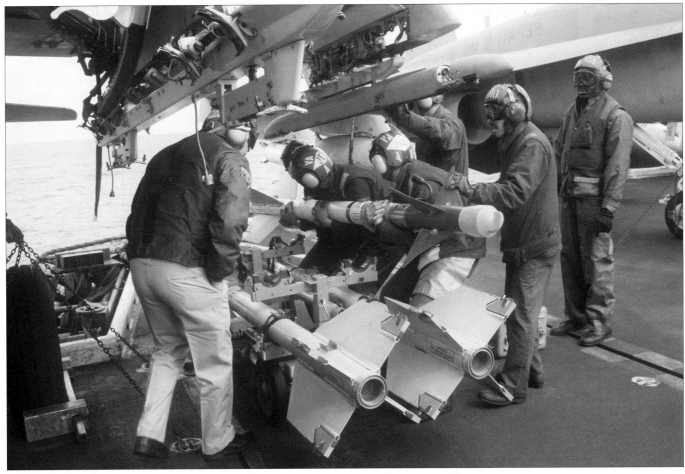

Weapon handlers loading an AIM-9L Sidewinder air-to-air missile to an A-6E from VA-55. Most of the back-breaking work of weapons-loading in the USN is still done by sheer muscle power. (US Navy photo)

It was the first deployment of the HARM and the decision was taken to make use of operational check opportunity for this new store. Nibe validated HARM's capability by nailing the SA-5's Square Pair radar.

On the Libyan side, operators of the SA-5 site saw the targets of two missiles they had fired in the meantime 'disappearing' from the display, which prompted them to conclude that they had destroyed two USN aircraft – raising the total of their claims for that evening to five. Following 'precise and objective analysis', Soviet instructors concluded that three US aircraft were destroyed.[76] Once again, no US aircraft were hit: USN pilots studied the SA-5 very carefully and knew how to avoid it by flying descending spirals to low altitude, below the horizon of Square Pair radar. If the fire-control radar of the site could not track them

– because of the Earth's curvature – missiles could not hit them, and that is what happened.

Apparently expecting darkness to provide them with an advantage, the Libyan Navy meanwhile continued deploying its FACMs into the Gulf of Syrte. The next clash began around 2150, when the E-2C supporting the SUCAPs and USS *Yorktown* detected a Project 1234E (ASCC-code Nanuchka II) -class missile corvette *Ean Mara* (hull number 416) heading west from the port of Benghazi. Although the six P-15 Termit (ASCC-code SS-N-2C Styx) anti-ship missiles carried by this vessel belonged to the first generation of such weapons, they still represented a serious threat for the USN. Correspondingly, two A-6Es from VA-85 were vectored to intercept. The Rockeye CBUs released by Intruders completely demolished *Ean Mara*'s radars and other electronics, and badly damaged the superstructure, but *Ean Mara* remained steerable. Before two other Intruders could re-attack her with Harpoons, her skipper manoeuvred the damaged corvette towards a nearby merchant ship. Realising a potential danger for neutral shipping, USN pilots aborted their attack and *Ean Mara* was left to return to Benghazi, which it reached early in the morning of 25 March.[77]

The following two engagements occurred around midnight and remain quite unclear to this day. Reacting to reports from F-14-crews of VF-33 that were underway on CAP Station 5 – north of Misurata – that they were fired upon by small arms and anti-aircraft artillery, and acquired by fire-control radars 'nearby', guided missile cruiser *Richmond K Turner* (CG-20) approached the Libyan coast to investigate. Around 2350, the cruiser made an unidentified surface contact to the south-west, at a range of 50 miles (80.5km) and engaged it with one RGM-84A Harpoon, claiming a hit on a Libyan Combattante II-class vessel. However, the E-2C that tracked this engagement reported no radar contact and a pair of A-6E Intruders that visually inspected the area also found nothing, and thus it remains unclear at exactly what the US cruiser opened fire.[78]

Red shirts' with a trolley loaded with three Mk.20 Rockeye cluster bomb units to load one of the A-6E Intruders from VA-55 on USS *Coral Sea* in March 1986. (US Navy photo)

Armed with an AGM-88A High-speed Anti-Radar Missile (HARM), this A-7E Corsair II from VA-83 is in the process of repositioning prior to its next launch cycle. The VA-83 led both attacks on the SA-5 SAM-site near Syrte. (US Navy photo)

The situation was similar in the case of a target tracked by the cruiser *Yorktown* since around 2300. The object in question was approaching at slow speed, and a pair of A-6Es on SUCAP were sent to investigate, but could not find anything. A few minutes after midnight, the same contact appeared to be making a turn for the centre of Task Force Zulu, straight for the *Coral Sea* that was in the process of refuelling from the tanker *Detroit* (AOE-4). At that time, *Yorktown* fired two RGM-84As from a range of about 11 miles (17.7km) and – after sonar operators reported two loud detonations from the corresponding position – claimed the destruction of an Italian-built, Assad-class corvette of the Libyan Navy (usually armed with four Otomat Teseo Mk.1 or Mk.2 anti-ship missiles and one 76mm calibre Otobreda cannon). Subsequent investigation by USN intelligence concluded that the operators of *Yorktown*'s SPY-1 radar system actually misclassified an aerial contact as surface target.[79]

Meanwhile, the SA-5 SAM-site near Syrte was repaired and online again, and four A-7Es from VA-83 deployed to re-attack it. Operating in similar fashion as the earlier attack, with a high-flying pair acting as bait while the other approached at low altitude, Corsairs fired two HARMs and knocked out both Square Pair radars of the SA-5 site. Although Libyan crews worked feverishly and repaired all damage by the following morning, the site was not reactivated. USN aircraft were thus free to roam the Gulf of Syrte for the rest of the night.

The End of *Ein Zaquit*

The final chapter of Operation Prairie Fire began around 0600 on 25 March 1986, when an E-2C detected what was initially assessed as another Combattante IIG-class FACM as it exited the port of Benghazi at a speed of 25 knots (46.3kmph). Believing they were up against a vessel not equipped with SAMs, the crew of an A-6E from VA-55 attacked and dropped two Rockeye CBUs. It was only then that the Libyan warship was properly identified as *Ein Zaquit* (hull number 419) – a Nanuchka-II-class missile corvette, equipped with SA-N-4 SAMs.[80] Although causing some damage, the bomblets failed to ignite the vessel and it continued at a high speed, prompting the Americans to presume it was still fully operational. A pair of Harpoon-armed A-6Es from VA-85 was then vectored to intercept. As these approached through the darkness of early morning, the bombardier/navigator of the lead Intruder located the Libyan warship with Norden AN/APQ-148 multi-mode radar, and then with the Target Recognition and Attack Multi-Sensor (TRAM) turret underneath the nose of the aircraft. The bombardier/navigator then called the nearby E-2C Hawkeye for permission to fire the only Harpoon his aircraft carried. The Hawkeye, in direct contact with the surface warfare commander aboard the *Saratoga*, replied, 'Affirmative, you have clearance to attack.' The bombardier/navigator then entered target's position, speed and heading into the Harpoon's homing head and launched the missile. After dropping from the A-6E, the small turbo-jet activated and carried the weapon as it hugged the sea for more than 30 miles – still outside the range of SAMs

carried by the Libyan vessel, as recalled by the pilot who fired it:

> That's a great advantage of having Harpoon. You can stay outside gun or missile range and not be in any danger of getting shoot at, yet still shoot and kill him … The shot went real smooth. The targeting and launch went just the way it was supposed to … It went in pretty quick and I doubt the Libyans saw it coming.[81]

The A-6E crew kept the Nanuchka in sight on their TRAM turret as the Harpoon skimmed ever closer:

> That morning was one of the clearest we had down there. In January and February every time we went down to the Gulf of Syrte the weather was terrible. It was windy, the sky was overcast, and the seas were high. But not that morning. Visibility was unlimited and after we hit the Nanuchka II, we could see its column of smoke 20 miles away.

Obviously not alerted to the attack, the crew of *Ean Zaquit* never reacted: the missile impacted the ship and detonated, causing the corvette to erupt in fire, smoke and debris. Flying about 500ft above the water, the two Intruders passed over the burning corvette before two A-6Es from the *Saratoga* delivered the *coup de grace* in the form of two Rockeye CBUs. As the ship went up in flames, survivors of the crew scrambled onto life rafts. Task Force Zulu did not interfere with Libyan search and rescue attempts. An Intruder-pilot from VA-55 subsequently observed:

> This attack was carried out within the SA-2 defensive ring, right off the beach, but no SAMs were launched because the A-6s stayed at 300 feet (91.44m) or lower! The MiGs stayed home too, even though we were pretty close to Benina air base.[82]

The sinking of *Ean Zaquit* was the last action of Operation Prairie Fire: although the USN continued operating inside and above the Gulf of Syrte for two days longer, and Tomcats, Hornets and Corsairs continued making high-speed runs towards the Libyan coast, their crews never heard another beep from the Libyans. Similarly, *Ticonderoga*, *Scott* and *Caron* steamed entirely unchallenged. Gaddafi's claim over the disputed waters and airspace was thus effectively destroyed.

Satisfied with the results of the battle, US Secretary of Defence Caspar Weinberger ordered Kelso to terminate Attain Document III on the afternoon of 27 March. By that time, Soviet advisors in Libya had recorded 480 sorties launched from the *America*, 336 from the *Coral Sea* and no less than 626 from the *Saratoga*.[83]

Unlike the French-run Operation Épervier in Chad, assessing the US-run Operations Attain Document I, II, and III, and Prairie Fire, is a much more complex task. Militarily, Prairie Fire in particular was an undisputed success, confirming that the billions spent by the Pentagon in research and development of new weapons, upgrades of existing aircraft, but especially in training of its officers, pilots and other personnel, were paying off. Deploying two, and then three CVBGs in the central Mediterranean, the USN confronted Libya with an air and sea-warfare system that the Libyan armed forces were unable to match. Aided by technologically superior combat support aircraft like the E-2C Hawkeye and EA-6B Prowler, excellently trained crews of the USN's F-14A Tomcats and F/A-18A Hornets repeatedly outmanoeuvred and outclassed their LAAF opponents who flew Mirage 5s, Mirage F.1s, MiG-23s and MiG-25s. The Americans proved disciplined enough not to open fire in any of about 180 engagements between them and the Libyans in January, February and March 1986, despite the often provocative behaviour of LAAF pilots. Because of this, USN pilots did not score any aerial victories. However, by repeatedly scoring 'mission kills' – in the form of denying freedom of operation to their opponents – they ultimately achieved a clear-cut victory for the skies over the Libyan-claimed Gulf of Syrte.

Because of that victory, the crews of USN A-6E Intruders and A-7E Corsair IIs were free to roam the skies during Operation Prairie Fire, and find, track, attack and destroy Libyan Navy vessels with ease. They also twice knocked out the dreaded SA-5 SAM-site near Syrte.

It is certain that neither the Libyan Arab Air Force, nor ground-based air defences or the Libyan Navy ever found any kind of working solution against this demonstration of power by the US Navy. Serious organisational shortcomings, deficiencies in training and operations in general, and – indeed – plentiful wishful thinking within the Libyan military were exposed fully, and it is unsurprising that Tripoli was left with no solution but to assume a strict defensive posture from very early on during Operation Prairie Fire.

Nevertheless, the sudden withdrawal of Task Force Zulu had offered Gaddafi an opportunity to claim a victory for Libya. Worse still, as events of the following days and weeks were to show, the entire US effort proved in vain because Operations Attain Document I, II and III, and Prairie Fire, all failed to deliver a blow against even a single objective related to international terrorism.

A-6E modex AA501 from VA-85 was one of the Intruders that sunk the Nanuchka-II-class missile corvette *Ein Zaquit* off the coast of Libya in the early morning of 25 March 1986. (US Navy photo)

Two stills from a TRAM-video taken by A-6Es from VA-85, showing the fiercely burning *Ein Zaquit* in the process of sinking, early on 25 March 1986. (US Navy release)

BIBLIOGRAPHY

Much of the material presented in this book was obtained in the course of research for the book series 'Arab MiGs', which presents the history of Arab air forces at war with Israel. Additional information was acquired during interviews with participants and eyewitnesses mentioned in the Acknowledgments and elsewhere, in Egypt and Libya, but also in France, the USA, Iraq and Syria. Sadly, earlier – *very serious and very direct* – threats against the security of specific persons prevented most of them from speaking openly, while the availability of original Libyan documentation remains very limited. Nevertheless, contributions of all persons who provided their recollections proved precious and enabled the authors to cross-examine the following publications (as well as those mentioned in footnotes) that were consulted in the preparation of this book:

Allam-Mi, A., *Tchad en Guerre: Tractations politiques et diplomatiques, 19751990* (Paris: L'harmattan, 2014).

Beaumont, H., *Mirage III, Mirage 5, Mirage 50: Toutes les versions en France et dans le Monde* (Clichy Cedex: Larivière, 2005, ISBN 2-84890-079-2).

Bévillard, General A., *La Saga du Transport Aérien Militaire Francais, De Kolwezi à Mazar-e-Sharif, de Port au Prince à Dumont-d'Urville, Tome 1* (Sceaux: l'Esprit du Livre Editions, 2007).

Blundy, D. and Lycett, A., *Qaddafi and the Libyan Revolution*, (Boston: Little Brown & Co, 1987, ISBN 978-0-316-10042-7).

Brent, W., *African Air Forces* (Nelspruit, South Africa:Freeworld Publications, 1999).

Chambost, G., *Missions de guerre: Histoires authentiques* (Paris: Altipresse, 2003, ISBN 978-2911218255).

Chenel, B., Liébert, M. and Moreau, E., *Mirage III/5/50 en service à l'étranger* (Hammeau Les Farges: LELA Presse, 2014).

Collectif, *Chronique du Charles de Gaulle; L'apogée d'un siècle d'aéronautique navale* (Chroniques Them, ISBN 978-2205053234).

Collectif, *Les avions de Renseignement Electronique, 50 ans d'activités secrètes racontées par les acteurs* (Paris: Lavauzelle/Association Guerrelec, 2009).

Collectif, *Le Jaguar dans ses Missions de Guerre Electronique* (Paris: Lavauzelle/Association Guerrelec, 2007).

Cooper, T., 'Darfur – Krieg der Antonow Bomber', *Fliegerrevue Extra* magazine (Germany), Vol. 20 (March 2008).

Cooper, T., Nicolle, D., with Nordeen, L., Salti, P. and Smisek, M., *Arab MiGs Volume 4: Attrition War, 19671973* (Houston: Harpia Publishing, 2013, ISBN 978-0-9854554-1-5).

Cooper, T., 'Tschad: Hintergründe', script for briefing on situation in Chad, delivered to the Offiziersgesellschaft Wien, 3 April 2008 (Austria).

Cooper, T., '45 Years of Wars and Insurgencies in Chad', *Truppendienst* magazine (Austria), Vol. 6 (2009).

Cooper, T., Weinert, P., Hinz, F. and Lepko, M., *African MiGs, MiGs and Sukhois in Service in Sub-Saharan Africa, Volume 1: Angola to Ivory Coast* (Vienna: Harpia Publishing, 2010, ISBN 978-0-9825539-5-4).

Cooper, T., Weinert, P., Hinz, F. and Lepko, M., *African MiGs, MiGs and Sukhois in Service in Sub-Saharan Africa, Volume 2: Madagascar to Zimbabwe* (Vienna: Harpia Publishing, 2011, ISBN 978-0-9825539-8-5).

Dini, M., 'Istruivo I Libici per conto di Roma', *Europeo Journal*, 28 July 1990.

Drendel, L., *Intruder* (Carrollton: Squadron/Signal Publications Inc., 1991, ISBN 0-89747-263-2).

Ernesto, Fabrizio Di, *Portaerei Italia: Sessant'anni di NATO nel nostro Paese* (Milan: Fuoco Edizioni, 2011).

Faligot, R., Guisnel, J. and Kauffer, R., *Histoire Politique des Services Secrets Français, de la Seconde Guerre Mondiale à nos Jours* (Paris: La Découverte, 2012).

Flintham, V., *Air Wars and Aircraft: a Detailed Record of Air Combat 1945 to the Present* (London: Arms and Armour Press, 1989, ISBN 0-85368-779-X).

Forget, General M., *Nos forces aériennes en Opex, Un demi-siècle d'intervention extérieures* (Paris: Economica, 2013).

Huertas, S. M., *Dassault-Bréguet Mirage III/5* (London: Osprey Publishing, 1990, ISBN 0-85045-933-8).

Irra, M., *The History of the Czechoslovak 1st Fighter Regiment, 19441994* (in Czech), (Ceskych Budejovicich Muzeum, 2014).

Koldunov, A., Chief Marshal of the Aviation, '*Information from Air Force Marshal Koldunov on issues related to US Aggression Against Libya, GVS-No.: A 456 721, EIGVS 819186*' (translation by Grace Leonard, extracted from the website of the Parallel History Project about the Cold War between NATO and the Warsaw Pact, www.isn.ethz.ch, in 2002).

Kotlobovskiy, A. B., *MiG-21 in Local Wars* (in Russian), (Kiev: ArchivPress, 1997).

Liébert, M. and Buyck, S., *Le Mirage F1 et les Mirage de seconde generation à voilure en fleche, Vol.1*: Projets et Prototypes (Outreau: Éditions Lela Presse, ISBN 2-914017-40-5).

Liébert, M. and Buyck, S., *Le Mirage F1 et les Mirage de seconde generation à voilure en fleche, Vol.2*: Les Mirage F1 de série, Un avion aux multiples facettes (Outreau: Éditions Lela Presse, ISBN 2-914017-41-3).

Lorell, Mark A., *Airpower in Peripheral Conflict: The French Experience in Africa* (Santa Monica: RAND, 1989, ISBN 0-8330-0937-0).

Mantoux, S., *Les guerres du Tchad (1969–1987)* (Clermont-Ferrand: Lemme edit Illustoria, 2014, ISBN 978-2-917575-49-9).

Martini, F., 'Sigonella 1985 – Cosi fermammo gli USA', *La Repubblica Journal*, 16 April 2003.

Nicoli, R., *Cocardi Tricolori Speciale 2: F-104S* (Novara: RN Publishing, 2007).

Nicoli, R., *Corardi Tricolori Speciale 4: F-104G* (Novara: RN Publishing, 2010).

Ougartchinska, R. and Priore, R., *Pour la Peau de Kadhafi*: Guerres, Secrets, et Mensonges, l'Autre Histoire (Paris: Fayard, Paris, 2010).

Piccinno, C. and Testa, P. P., 'La strana storia dei pilot di Gheddafi', *Avvenimenti Journal*, 27 July 1993.

Pollack, Kenneth M., *Arabs at War: Military Effectiveness, 19481991* (Lincoln, Nebraska: University of Nebraska Press, 2004, ISBN 0-8032-8783-6).

Protti, D. and Provvisionato, S., 'Nemico, ti insegno a uccidere', *Europeo Journal*, 21 July 1990.

Sené, F., *Raids Dans le Sahara Central Tchad Libye 1941–1987: Sarra Ou le Rezzou Decisif* (Paris: L'Harmattan, 2011, ISBN 978-2296566446).

Sergievsky, A., 'Fire in the Prairie' (in Russian), *VKO Magazine*, No. 4/17 (2004).

Sharpe. Captain R., *Jane's Fighting Ships 1992–1993* (Coulsdon: Jane's Information Group Ltd., 1992, ISBN 0-7106-0983-3).

Stafrace, C., *Arab Air Forces* (Carolton: Squadron/Signal Publications Inc., 1994, ISBN 0-89747-326-4).

Stafrace, C., *The Air Campaign for the Freedom of Libya, February to October 2011, Operations Odyssey Dawn and Unified Protector* (Camouflage & Markings Number 6) (Bletchley: Guideline Publications, 2012).

Stanik, Joseph T., *El Dorado Canyon: Reagan's Undeclared War with Qaddafi* (Annapolis: Naval Institute Press, ISBN 1-55750-983-2).

Storaro, F., *1964–1984: Vent'anni di Aeronautica Militare – Missione Africa* (Rome: Instituto Bibliografico Napoleone, 2010).

Thompson, Sir R. (ed.), *War in Peace: An Analysis of Warfare since 1945* (London: Orbis Publishing, 1981, ISBN 0-85613-341-8).

Turner, J. W., *Continent Ablaze: The Insurgency Wars in Africa 1960 to the Present* (London: Arms & Armour Press, 1998, ISBN 1-85409-128-X).

Valente, D. and Pozzi, P., *Lockheed-Aeritalia F-104 Starfighter* (Milan: Intergest, 1976).

Vezin, Alain, *Jaguar, le félin en action* (Boulogne: ETAI, 2008).

Willis, D. (ed.), *Aerospace Encyclopaedia of World Air Forces* (London: Aerospace Publishing Ltd., 1999, ISBN 1-86184-045-4).

World Defence Almanac, *Military Technology* magazine volumes 1/91, 1/93, 1/95, 1/97, 1/98 and 1/03.

Zaloga, Steven J., *Red SAM: The SA-2 Guideline Anti-Aircraft Missile* (Oxford: Osprey Publishing Ltd, 2007, ISBN 978-1-84603-062-8).

Zolotaryov, Major General V. A., *Russia in Local Wars and Military Conflicts in the Second Half of the 20th Century* (in Russian) (Moscow: Institute of Military History, Ministry of Defence of the Russian Federation, 2000).

Various volumes of *El-Djeich* Magazine (the official publication of the Algerian Ministry of Defence), *Air Fan, le Fana de l'Aviation, Aviation Magazine Internationale, Air et Cosmos*, and *Raids* (France), *Aviation News* magazine (UK), and personal notes of all the authors based on other various daily and weekly printed publications.

ACKNOWLEDGEMENTS

The authors wish to express their special gratitude to all those individuals who contributed to this book. Foremost are several former Libyan air force pilots who were forced to leave their country because of issues related to their own safety, and that of their family. Some of them have granted interviews only on condition of anonymity, and thus we feel free here only to forward our special thanks for providing advice, unique information and insights to Abdoul Hassan, Ali Tani and Hazem al-Bajigni.

Several retired US Navy pilots and officers have kindly provided advice and interviews too, although – again because of clear, direct and very specific threats for their personal security – they also felt forced to do so on condition of anonymity. The exception we feel free to mention is Dave 'Hey Joe' Parsons, to whom we wish to express our special thanks.

We would also like to thank several retired French Air Force pilots, servicemen and members of their families, who kindly provided permission to use their documentation, family archives and photographs.

Other thanks go to a number of researchers elsewhere, who kindly helped during the work on this book, in particular: Group 73 and friends in Egypt; Brigadier-General Ahmad Sadik from Iraq; Dr David Nicolle in Great Britain; Tom Long in the USA; Arthur Hubers and Jeroen Nijemeijer from the Netherlands; Roberto Giovanetti and Leonardo Pinzauti from Italy; Robert Szombati from Hungary; Javier Nat from Spain; Vaclav Havner, Josef Simon, and Miroslav Irra from the Czech Republic; Milos Sipos from Slovakia; Pit Weinert from Germany; and Christof Hahn from Austria. All of them provided extensive aid in one or other form of related research and eventually made this book possible.

(Endnotes)

1. While theoretically considered equivalent to an NCO rank in the USA or Great Britain, the French rank of Aspirant and Major is actually in between officer and NCO ranks, and considered the lowest officer rank, though also the highest NCO rank.

2. Excerpts from various AdA Intelligence Monthly Bulletins from the period JanuaryNovember 1977, provided on condition of anonymity.

3. Documentazione Tecnico Formale; Informazioni Supplementari (Incivolo velivolo libico MiG-23MS; 18 luglio 1980 Capt Pil EZZEDEN Khalil; Timpa dele Megere presso CASTELSILANO), Volumes 1 and 2, pp. 4,079, 4,102, 4,346.

4. Ibid, pp. 4,122, 4,138, 4,140.

5. Ibid, pp. 4,095, 4,153; Daniele Biacchessi & Fabrizio Colarieti, *Punto Condor, Ustica: il processo* (Pendragon, 2002; ISBN 88-8342-134-5), p. 51.

6. Documentazione Tecnico Formale, Vols 1 & 2.

7. Ibid, Vol.2, p. 4,339.

8. Commander Henry Kleeman was killed – but years later: he piloted the F/A-18 of the USN squadron VX-4 that turned turtle following an aqua-planing-related landing accident at Naval Air Station (NAS) Miramar, in California (USA), on 3 December 1985. Kleeman's RIO from air combat with Libyan Sukhois on 19 August 1981, Lieutenant David J. Venlet, is still serving with the USN: in January 2015, he was the Program Executive Officer for the F-35 Lightning II Program, with the rank of Vice Admiral.

9. R. Ougartchinska and R. Priore, *Pour la Peau de Kadhafi*, p.121; *L'Unita Journal*, 29 September 1978. According to Ougartchinska, the OSI-SA sometimes provided its own services for such operations – as in the case of former Green Beret operative Eugene Tafoya, who gunned down a Libyan dissident living in Colorado, USA. In other cases, cooperation between Tripoli, Tespil and Wilson went much further. In 1978, the Libyans decided to request OSI-SA to recruit and train a mixed commando force of Western mercenaries and Tobou insurgents loyal to Gaddafi for an attack on the international airport outside the Chadian capital of N'Djamena, where they were expected to destroy any French aircraft. The Americans hired two French mercenaries for this operation – Roland Raucoules and Michel Winter – and ordered them to find and buy a French-registered transport aircraft for a 'covert operation somewhere in Africa'. Raucoules and Winter found an old Uni Air Douglas DC-3, and on 21 June 1978 contracted its pilot, Philippe Toutut. In September of the same year, Toutut was requested to fly a load consisting of ten drums of fuel and a fuel pump from Sicily to northern Chad. Only once he landed near Zouar, in the Tibesti range, was the Frenchman informed about his actual mission: landing an aircraft full of commandos at N'Djamena IAP. Not only Toutut but also Raucoules and Winter protested vehemently. After lengthy discussions, they acted as if in agreement with Libyan plot and agreed to go. In fact, the three French then escaped with the aircraft and reported this plan to the French authorities in Chad.

10. See Part 1, p. 20 for Libyan narrative about this affair. In the USA, this affair was revealed to the public in 1981. It resulted in the arrest of Wilson and his sentencing to 22 years in prison. In Great Britain, a related affair became known only in 1983, when it turned out that Stubbs attempted to help the LAAF obtain several Lockheed L-100s from Australia.

11. Sources about military cooperation between Czechoslovakia and Libya include interviews with Vaclav Havner, Milos Sipos, Josef Simon and Miroslav Irra, and Irra's book, *The History of the Czechoslovak 1st Fighter Regiment, 1944–1994* (in Czech) (Ceskych Budejovicich Muzeum, 2014).

12. OT-62 was a Czechoslovak variant of the Soviet-made BTR-50 APC. Together with T-55s and BTR-50s, Czechoslovaks also delivered a small number of Soviet-made T-34/85 medium tanks that were used for training purposes. The deal in question eventually frustrated French efforts to sell their AMX-30 MBTs to Libya.

13. The first of the Czechoslovak-trained Libyan students was certified as qualified in April 1979.

14. Similar to their Yugoslav colleagues, several Czechoslovak instructors who used to serve in Libya recall often 'absurd occurrences', caused by the lack of motivation of their Libyan cadets. They all recalled the discipline as 'very harsh', 'including physical punishment'.

15. Libyan Arab Army cadets attended courses at the Czechoslovak Army Academy 'Antonin Zapotocky' in Brno.

16. As the living conditions improved over time, many Czechoslovak instructors deployed in Libya began bringing their families with them. Apartments provided for them differed, from good accommodations at bases in the main coastal cities, like Tripoli and Syrte, to rather Spartan, mobile homes at in-land air bases such as al-Wigh and Brach. The number of Czechoslovak civilians grew to a degree where Czechoslovak schools had to be set up to accommodate their children.

17. Czechoslovaks were fully aware of the nature of most such organisations and clearly labelled them as 'terrorists' in their reports.

18. This agreement resulted in a Libyan order for 1,500 upgrade kits known as 'Kladivo' (Hammer) for Libyan MBTs. These primarily included a much more modern fire-control system (FCS) and additional turret armour for Libyan T-55s. However, implementation of this project was hampered by subsequent difficulties: only 10 Klavido kits were delivered and very little related work was undertaken in Libya.

19. This and the following two sub-chapters are based on Storaro, *Missione Africa*; Piccinno & Testa, *La strana storia dei piloti di Gheddafi*;

Protti & Provvisionato, *Nemico, ti insegno a uccidere*; Valante & Pozzi, *Lockheed-Aeritalia F-104 Starfighter*; Di Ernesto, *Portaerei Italia*; Dini, *Istuivo I Libici per conto di Roma*; and Nicoli, *Cocardi Tricolori Speciale*. For details on all these publications, see Bibliography.

20. As well as aircraft, Libya purchased large amounts of other armament from Italy, including four corvettes of al-Assad-class, 10 (French-built) Combatante II-class fast missile craft, 220 Otomat surface-to-surface (or anti-ship) missiles and an unknown quantity of Aspide surface-to-air missiles. Furthermore, the Libyan Arab Army acquired 200 FH-70 Palmaria 155mm calibre self-propelled howitzers, 50 M113 APCs carrying 120mm calibre mortars, an unknown number of Type 6614 armoured cars and 16 Bofors L/70 40mm calibre anti-aircraft cannons.

21. The designation 'Atlantic' was used for the first version of Bréguet Br.1150, sold to France, Germany, Italy, the Netherlands and Pakistan. The second variant was manufactured for Aéronavale (French Naval Aviation) only, and designated Atlantique (also 'ATL2'). It entered service in 1991.

22. Attrition of LAAF Mirage 5 units was heavy: at least 17 were written off in different accidents in the 1970s and 1980s, while four were shot down during the October 1973 Arab-Israeli War while on loan to Egypt. For details see, Ougartchinska et al, p. 38; Chenel et al, pp. 198-203, 206-207, 209-210; and Cooper et al, *Arab MiGs Volumes 4, 5* and *6*.

23. Koldunov, *Information*, p. 2.

24. Despite persistent rumours at the time that Nicaragua was about to receive MiG-21 interceptors – either from Cuba or the USSR – the Sandinista government subsequently declared that it had no previous knowledge of this shipment. The Brazilians initially impounded all four transports and their cargo, before returning them to Libya a few weeks later.

25. Stanik, pp. 81-83.

26. Stanik, pp. 83-84.

27. Director of Central Intelligence, 'Libya's Qadhafi: The Challenge to US and Western Interests, Special National Intelligence Estimate 36.5-85', *CIA*, March 1985, p. 5.

28. William E Smith, 'Terror Aboard Flight 847', *Time Magazine*, 24 June 2001.

29. It is notable that Israel officially denied that the prisoners' release was related to the hijacking. Similarly, Hezbollah denied any involvement in the hijacking of TWA Flight 847. The aircraft was held by the Lebanese authorities at Beirut IAP until 16 August 1985.

30. Wolf Blitzer, 'Pollard: Not A Bumbler, but Israel's Master Spy', *The Washington Post*, 15 February 1987; Edwin Black, 'Does Jonathan Pollard Deserve a Life Sentence?', *History News Network*, 20 June 2002. Pollard is known to have provided satellite reconnaissance photographs of the PLO HQ in Tunisia and details on the capabilities of Libyan air defences.

31. Italian authorities granted permission for the Israelis to overfly Italian territory during this mission.

32. Frank J. Prial, 'Tunisia's Leader Bitter at the US', *New York Times*, 3 October 1985; Patrick Seale, *Abu Nidal: A Gun for Hire* (London: Arrow, 1993); Shlomo Aloni, *Israeli F-15 Eagle Units in Combat* (Oxford: Osprey Publishing Ltd, 2006), pp. 67-69.

33. Since the independence of Croatia (internationally recognised in 1992), Dubrovnik is one of the southern-most cities and ports in Croatia.

34. Witherspoon, 'Tomcat Sunset Symposium', *Oceana*, Sept. 2006; this and all subsequent quotations from Witherspoon are based on his presentation during the same symposium.

35. Designations of Italian Air Force's Gruppos used to be written in Latin numbers at the time.

36. Interview with one of the involved Italian pilots granted on condition of anonymity, May 2001.

37. & Stanik, p. 101-103.

38. Contrary to widespread belief, USS *Coral Sea* was perfectly capable of operating heavier aircraft too, including F-14 Tomcats. Indeed, time and again through the 1980s, the ship hosted Tomcat squadrons that were undergoing their 'car quals' (carrier qualifications).

39. Stumpf, pp. 42, 44.

40. US narratives about Attain Document confirm that a 'flight of several MiG-25s' passed over *Coral Sea* but, 'with F/A-18s closely escorting them, the Libyans wisely elected not to make any threatening moves'. See Stanik, p. 125.

41. Most of the missions in question were flown by one of four Mirage IVAs usually assigned to the 1st Squadron of the Centre for Instruction of Strategic Air Forces (Centre d'Instruction Forces Aériennes Stratégiques, CIFAS). For this purpose, these bombers carried one of eight CT.52 reconnaissance pods packed with cameras (and, if necessary, an infra-red line-scanner) delivered to the AdA. While such pods could actually be carried by any of the Mirage IVAs in service, they are not to be confused with the dedicated reconnaissance variant, Mirage IVP, which entered service only in May 1986.

42. Ahmad Allam-Mi, pp. 250, 298; Turner, p. 172.

43. Ahmad Allam-Mi, pp. 250, 298.

44. Ibid, p. 282.

45. Ibid, pp. 200-201.

46. Ibid, pp. 170-171.

47. Ibid, pp. 200-201.

48. Faligot et al, pp. 31419; Ahmad Allam-Mi, pp. 250, 298.

49. Ahmad Allam-Mi, pp. 117-119.

50. Vezin, pp. 141-142.

51. Originally designed as maritime patrol aircraft with good anti-submarine capabilities, the Atlantics in question were slightly more than this. Back in the early 1970s, France began work on developing an indigenous AWACS aircraft. The original ideas were based on the airframe of the Airbus A300B wide-body airliner, while a cheaper variant envisaged the use of the C.160 Transall. Insufficient funding eventually led to the cancellation of this project. Instead, the French began experimenting with their Atlantics and also equipped these for ELINT/SIGINT-gathering purposes (some of this work subsequently resulted in the above-mentioned Atlantique or ATL2 variant). That is why Atlantics drawn from the 21 and 22 Flottilles of the French Naval Aviation (Aéronavale) began regularly deploying to Chad during Opération Tacaud in 1981. Of course, calling them 'AWACS' would have been a long stretch: in regular service, Atlantics remained foremost MPAs, with good ELINT/SIGINT-gathering capability as a secondary task. However, because their Iguane radar proved capable of detecting and tracking even small targets over considerable distances, they began serving as quasi-AEW aircraft during Opération Épervier.

52. Vezin, pp. 14142; Cooper et al, *Libyan Air Wars, Part 1*, pp. 56, 64.

53. 'Chad Seeks French Aid Against Libyan Attack', *New York Times*, 14 February 1986.

54. Vezin, pp. 143-144.

55. Post-strike intelligence, apparently acquired via the Libyan embassy in Bangui, revealed that Wadi Doum AB suffered the loss of all electric power during the previous night. The exact reason remains unknown.

56. Ahmad Allam-Mi, p. 283; Vezin, pp. 143-144; Flintham, p. 95; Turner, p. 173.

57. Jaguar A91 suffered no less than 10 hits, the worst of which cracked the windshield. Two others damaged the IFR-probe and the third internal fuel tank behind the pilot. The latter damage required removal of the wing to repair, which took nearly a month to accomplish with the help of tools available at Bangui IAP. Curiously, the same Jaguar was hit again by an Iraqi SA-7 MANPAD during the first AdA mission over Kuwait, in 1991 war against Iraq. It thus became the only modern-day AdA aircraft to be hit twice in war and each time return its pilot safely back to base.

58. Collectif, Le Jaguar dans ses Missions de Guerre Electronique, pp. 70-71, 187-194.

59. There is some controversy over the exact altitude from which the LAAF Tu-22 released its bombs to hit the runway of N'Djamena IAP. According to General Bertrand Litre (interview to AFP-Sahara, published on 20 February 1986, p. 60), it did so from an altitude of 5,000m (16,404ft). Most other sources describe altitudes between 300 and 500m (between 984 and 1,640ft). French air traffic controller Claude Roussel saw the Tupolev briefly emerging from the morning mist and apparently manoeuvring as if it would attempt a landing. His recollection was confirmed by Chadian Minister of Information Mahamat Soumaila in an interview with the local media, who said the bomber descended to only 300m above the runway and had simulated an emergency landing during the attack (see Florent Sené, *Raids dans le Sahara central: Tchad, Libye, 1941–1987*).

60. According to Roumiana Ougartchinska and Rosario Priore in *Pour la Peau de Kadhafi* (pp. 145-159), the Libyan Tu-22 that bombed N'Djamena IAP was shot down by French flak. The AdA subsequently deployed a commando team to inspect the crash site and wreckage, which appears to have been well north of the 16th Parallel. The French commandos found the bodies of the crew too, and – reportedly – these were not Libyans, but of 'East European origin'. While some Western sources have cited them as East Germans, the authors' research in this direction ended inconclusively. Not only was there no trace of any kind of involvement of the East German air force or intelligence on the side of Libya during the war in Chad, the fact is that the former East German air force did not operate any Tu-22 bombers, but only aircraft with such a short range that most of them would have been unable to reach even parts of West Germany covered by German and US MIM-23B I-HAWK SAM-sites. There was no reason for East Germans to become involved in the operations of Libyan Tu-22s.

61. Contrary to earlier such missions, this variant was selected for its relatively better fuel consumption and a more precise INS nav/attack platform in comparison to the Mirage IVP.

62. Collectif, *Les Avions de Renseignment Electronique*, p. 155. When jettisoning drop tanks, the Mirage IV also jettisoned pylons for these. Interestingly, although Phimat ECM pods entered service with Mirage IVAs in 1984 (and Barracuda ECM pods entered service with Mirage IVPs in 1986), during this mission, the aircraft depended on its high speed, high operational altitude and two internal ECM systems for protection from Libyan SAMs. The Mygale ARAB-6B system was specially tuned to jam the SA-3s, and Agasol ARAD-31A to jam the SA-6.

63. Ironically, Paris did consider buying some C-141s, in 1967, but plans were axed due to lack of necessary funding.

64. Stanik, pp. 12729.

65. Ibid, p. 131.

66. Ougartchinska and Priore, *Pour la Peau de Kadhafi*, p. 88.

67. Koldunov, 'Information', p. 1.

68. 'Operation Prairie Fire', VKO, No. 4/17, 2004.

69. Koldunov, 'Information', p. 1.

70. Operation Prairie Fire', VKO, No. 4/17, 2004.

71. Koldunov, 'Information', p. 2. It is notable that US intelligence was right when assessing that the SA-5 battery at Syrte operated under Gaddafi's direct authority; see Stanik, p. 132.

72. Stanik, p. 133.

73. Ibid, p. 134.

74. *Jane's Fighting Ships 199293* (p. 379) credited Otomat Teseus Mk. 2 missiles with range of 80km (43.2 miles), but this was possible only with the help of mid-course guidance, provided with the support of an airborne platform – such as a reconnaissance aircraft or helicopter – which in this case was not available.

75. 'The Year in Review, 1986', *Naval Aviation News* No. 69, JulyAugust 1987.

76. Koldunov, 'Information', p. 2.

77. Stanik, p. 137; *Ean Mara* was repaired in Leningrad, in the former USSR, and returned to Libya in early 1991 under the name *Tariq Ibn Ziyad*.

78. Stanik, p. 137; in comparison, *Jane's Fighting Ships 199293* (p. 379) reported one of the Libyan Combattante IIG-class FACMs as 'severely damaged on 25 March 1986 by forces of the US Sixth Fleet'.

79. Stanik, p. 137. While some sources state that the Libyan Navy did lose an Assad-class corvette that night – namely the vessel *Assad al-Tadjier* (hull number 412) – this remains unconfirmed. Only one of the ships in question (*Assad al-Hudud*, hull number 415) was ever seen afterwards, while others were reportedly cannibalised for spares (see *Jane's Fighting Ships 1992-1993*, p. 379).

80. According to Stanik (p. 137), the USN actually misidentified this vessel as *Ean Mara*. It was only years later that it became known that *Ean Mara* was severely damaged during an earlier attack of A-6Es from VA-85, while the Nanuckha-II corvette attacked early in the morning of 25 March was actually *Ean Zaquit*.

81. Timothy J. Christmann, 'Harpoon Proves Its Tenacity: A-6Es Thump Libyan Combatants', *Naval Aviation News* No.68, JulyAugust 1986.

82. Drendel, p. 60.

83. 'Operation Prairie Fire', VKO, No. 4/17, 2004. Apart from the activity of carrier-borne aircraft, the Soviets tracked a number of sorties by aircraft they assessed as RC-135s, E-3A Sentry and even Lockheed SR-71 Blackbirds of the US Air Force. According to them, such aircraft usually patrolled about 100km off the Libyan coast.

Authors

Tom Cooper

Tom Cooper, from Austria, is a military-aviation analyst and historian. Following a career in worldwide transportation business – in which, during his extensive travels in Europe and the Middle East, he established excellent contacts – he moved into writing. An earlier fascination with post-Second World War military aviation has narrowed to focus on smaller air forces and conflicts, about which he has collected extensive archives of material. Concentrating primarily on air warfare that has previously received scant attention, he specialises in investigative research on little-known African and Arab air forces, as wella s the Iranian air force. Cooper has published 23 books – including the unique 'Arab MiGs' series, which examined the development and service history of major Arab air forces in conflicts with Israel – as well as over 250 articles on related topics, providing a window into a number of previously unexamined yet fascinating conflicts and relevant developments.

Albert Grandolini

Military historian and aviation-journalist, Albert Grandolini, was born in Vietnam and gained an MA in history from Paris I Sorbonne University. His primary research focus is on contemporary conflicts in general and particularly on the military history of Asia. Having spent his childhood in South Vietnam, the Vietnam War has been one of his main fields of research. He is the author of the books Fall of the Flying Dragon: South Vietnamese Air Force (1973–1975) with Harpia Publishing and the two volumes on Vietnam's Easter Offensive of 1972 with Helion Publishers in the Asia@War Series, and is also co-author of the three volumes of the Libyan Air Wars with Helion Publishers in the Africa@War Series. He has also written numerous articles for various British, French and German magazines, such as Air Enthusiast, Flieger Revue Extra, Fana de l'aviation, Tank Zone and Batailles et Blindés. He has regularly contributed to the Air Combat Information Group (ACIG) and the Au Delà de la Colline military history French website.

Arnaud Delalande

Arnaud Delalande is researcher and author from Tours in France. Military history, and the history of military aviation in particular have long been his passion, especially airpower in Africa and in former French colonies. Except for working as editor of 'Aéro Histo' blog (http://aerohisto.blogspot.fr) and contributor of 'Alliance Geostrategique' blog (alliancegeostrategique.org) in his spare time, he has become one of few foreigners with deeper interest in the history of recent Chadian wars, as well as French military operations in that country. He has published several related articles in specialized French magazines such as Air Fan, and Air Combat. He is also co-author of the three volumes of the Libyan Air Wars with Helion Publishers in the Africa@War Series.